THE INFANCY NARRATIVES

Rev. Francis R. Davis
St. Bernard's Seminary
2260 Lake Avenue
Rochester, New York 14612

Scripture for Meditation: 1

THE INFANCY NARRATIVES

by John Bligh

ST PAUL PUBLICATIONS

ST PAUL PUBLICATIONS,
LANGLEY, BUCKS., GREAT BRITAIN.

ST PAUL PUBLICATIONS,
BALLYKEERAN, ATHLONE, IRELAND.

© 1968 ST PAUL PUBLICATIONS

NIHIL OBSTAT: EDGAR HARDWICK PH. D., CENSOR DEPUTATUS, DIE 20A MAII 1968. IMPRIMATUR: + CHARLES GRANT L.C.L.M.A., BISHOP OF NORTHAMPTON, DIE 22A MAII 1968.

The "Nihil obstat" and "Imprimatur" are a declaration that a book or pamphlet is considered to be free from doctrinal or moral error. It is not implied that those who have granted the "Nihil obstat" and "Imprimatur" agree with the contents or statements expressed.

"The Bible text of the Old Testament in this publication is from the Revised Standard Version of the Holy Bible, Catholic Edition, copyright © 1965 and 1966 by the Division of Christian Education of the National Council of the Churches of Christ in the U.S.A. and used by permission."

FIRST PUBLISHED JULY 1968 BY ST PAUL PUBLICATIONS AND PRINTED IN ENGLAND BY SOCIETY OF ST PAUL, LANGLEY, BUCKINGHAMSHIRE.

CONTENTS

To Pray as We Ought	9
The Power of the Lord	14
The Lord is with you	19
The Ark of the Covenant	23
The New Name	28
The Two Censuses	32
No Room at the Inn	36
The Lamb of God	39
The Saviour is Born	43
The Heavenly Liturgy	48
The New Rachel	52
Nunc Dimittis	56
The End of the Law	60
The End of the Temple	65
Awaiting the Consolation of Israel	69
Wrestling with God	73
Anna and Mary	77
Beginning, Middle and End	81
A Cloud of Sadness	85
The true Son of David	90
Solomon and Jesus	95
Frankincense and Myrrh	99
The Suffering of the Innocent	104
The New Beginning	108

BURNS OATES
RETAIL
.-L 00-10-6T

1850 14 Nov

LONDON
THANK YO

Foreword

The gospels which include Infancy Narratives are those written by St Matthew and St Luke. St Mark and St John both begin from the ministry of John the Baptist (cf. Acts 1:22).

In this book, first the narratives of St Luke, then those of St Matthew are taken in consecutive sections; each section is preceded by another passage of Scripture (usually from the Old Testament) and is followed by a brief reflection or meditation; and finally a prayer is suggested.

The reader may be tempted to skip the Scripture readings and go straight to the reflection, on the ground that the readings are already well known to him. But however familiar they may be, it will be wiser to re-read them. The texts are chosen to cast light on each other, and the reflection assumes that the reader has them fresh in mind.

Nowadays, one often hears it said, despairingly, that since the Scripture scholars started applying the techniques of modern exegesis to the Infancy Narratives, no one can any longer draw a spiritual message from them without making himself look foolish. I trust this little book will help to correct this misapprehension.

John Bligh, S.J.

1
To pray as we ought

God's Message to Daniel

In the first year of Darius the son of Ahasuerus, by birth a Mede, who became king over the realm of the Chaldeans, in the first year of his reign, I, Daniel, perceived in the books the number of years which, according to the word of the Lord to Jeremiah the prophet, must pass before the end of the desolations of Jerusalem, namely, seventy years. Then I turned my face to the Lord God, seeking him by prayer and supplications with fasting and sackcloth and ashes ... While I was speaking and praying, confessing my sin and the sin of my people Israel, and presenting my supplication before the Lord my God for the holy hill of my God; while I was speaking in prayer, the man Gabriel, whom I had seen in the vision at the first, came to me in swift flight at the time of the evening sacrifice. He came to me and said to me, 'O Daniel, I have now come out to give you wisdom and understanding. At the beginning of your supplications a word went forth, and I have come to tell it to you, for you are greatly beloved; therefore consider the word and understand the vision. Seventy weeks of years are decreed concerning your people and your holy city, to finish the transgression, to put an end to sin, and to atone for iniquity, to bring in everlasting righteousness, to seal both vision and prophet, and to anoint a most holy one.'

(*Dan 9:1-3,20-24*)

God's Message to Zachary

In the days when Herod was king of Judaea, there was a priest named Zachary, of the Order of Abijah. His wife too was a descendant of Aaron, and her name was Elizabeth. Both were just in God's eyes, for they followed blamelessly all the commandments and ordinances of the Lord. But they had no children, for Elizabeth was barren, and both of them were advanced in years.

When it was his Order's turn of duty, Zachary was serving as priest in God's presence; lots were cast as usual, and it fell to Zachary to go in and offer the incense in the Lord's sanctuary. At the hour of the offering of incense, while great numbers of the people were praying outside, there appeared to Zachary an angel of the Lord, standing at the right hand of the altar of incense. Zachary was troubled by the sight and fear fell upon him. But the angel said to him: 'Have no fear, Zachary; thy prayer has been heard; thy wife Elizabeth will bear thee a son, and thou shalt name him John. He will bring joy and gladness to thee, and many will rejoice over his birth; for he will be great in the sight of the Lord. He will not drink wine or strong liquor, but will be filled with the Holy Spirit, even from his mother's womb. He will reconcile many of the children of Israel to the Lord their God. He will go before the Lord with the spirit and power of Elijah, to reconcile the hearts of fathers to their children, to convert the disobedient to the wisdom of just men, and to prepare for the Lord a people ready to receive him.'

Zachary said to the angel: 'But how shall I know whether this is true, I am an old man and my wife is advanced in years.' The angel replied: 'I am Gabriel, who stand in God's presence and am sent to speak to thee and to bring these good tidings. Behold, thou shalt be dumb and unable to speak until the day when these things come to pass, because thou hast not believed these words of mine, which will be proved true in their time.'

Meanwhile, the people were waiting for Zachary, and wondering why he lingered in the sanctuary. But when he came out and could not speak to them, they understood that he had seen a vision in the sanctuary. He made signs to them, but remained without speech.

When the days of his office were over, he returned home. After this, his wife Elizabeth conceived. For five months she preserved secrecy about herself, thinking: 'The Lord has done this for me; in these days he has looked upon me, and has taken away my reproach among men.'

(*Lk 1:5-25*)

Reflection

Since we do not know how to pray as we ought, we should listen attentively whenever the Scriptures have something to say about prayer. In the passage from Daniel, we see the prophet recognising his own ignorance and praying for understanding; then understanding is given to him. Is it not possible that we suppose too easily that we already understand what God has revealed? We often pray for grace to do this or to do that, but rarely for grace to understand.

Zachary in the temple had been praying before the angel appeared, and his prayer was heard. He had been praying for the consolation of his people Israel and for the coming of the Messiah—not a private prayer for his own spiritual advancement, but public prayer, offered for the whole people. Such a prayer deserved to be carried up by the angels into God's presence. Gabriel has come to announce its fulfilment: a child shall be born to Zachary, and he will be filled with the spirit of Elijah, to call the people back to the Law and make them ready to receive their Lord, the Anointed and Holy One.

Zachary's prayer began well, and won the angel's approval; but it ended less well. He foolishly asked for a further sign, although he had already been given one sign (the appearance of the angel) and promised another (the birth of a son in his old age). His request for a further sign sprang, not from faith, but from lack of it, and therefore met with punishment, in the form of dumbness, the first effect of which was that when he went out to meet the people of Jerusalem in the temple courts, he was unable to pronounce the blessing over them.

From this we may draw the lesson that it is better to pray for the Church and for others than for oneself, that God is ready to console his people if and when we ask, and that he does so by raising up men like John, filled with the spirit of Elijah, to call his people back to the way of their Lord and make them ready to encounter their Master on the Day of Judgment. St Paul was such a man—in many ways remarkably like John the Baptist. In every generation the Church has need of such men. One of the few things Christ taught about prayer was that we should ask the Lord of the harvest to send reapers into his fields—men to whom he has given gifts of understanding, of holiness, and of eloquent speech.

It is better to pray unselfishly for others than to be anxious about one's personal advancement in holiness, for all anxiety springs from lack of faith. Experience seems to show that anxious prayers for one's private advantage vanish down the wind. Perhaps the Jews were right: the angels exercise a censorship over our prayers; the good ones they deliver to the court of heaven, and the others they lose on the way. The Our Father, which, according to St Matthew, is to be said by each individual, in his private room, with the door shut, is nevertheless a community prayer for the needs of all members of the Church: '*Our* Father... deliver *us* from evil.'

In the early Church, Christians prayed earnestly for the return of the Lord in glory: 'Maranatha! Come, Lord Jesus!' But we, alas, are not ready for his coming. First we must work and pray for the reunion of divided Christendom: that all who invoke the name of Jesus may join together in one worshipping community, without any of the walls of partition which now sadden every Christian and scandalize the unbeliever. Here is a worthy prayer: that we all may be one!

Prayer

Heavenly Father, come to the assistance of your Church: raise up among us men who will know your will; give them wisdom and power to reunite your people and lead us back to the way of the commandments, and to the more perfect way of the Sermon on Mount, so that we may all be ready to meet in Judgment our Lord Jesus Christ your Son, who lives and reigns with you in the unity of the Holy Spirit, and is God, world without end. Amen.

2

The power of the Word

God's Message to the Romans

I give thanks to my God through Jesus Christ for what he has done for all of you; for your faith is renowned throughout the world. God is my witness, to whom I render spiritual service by preaching the gospel of his Son, that I remember you unceasingly, and constantly ask in my prayers that if God so wills, by some means, now at last I may have the chance to come to you. I am longing to see you, in order that I may impart to you some spiritual gift and so strengthen you—or rather, in order that we may encourage one another through the faith we see in one another, both yours and mine. I should like you to know, brethren, that although I have always hitherto been prevented, I have many times planned to visit you, in the hope that I may gather some fruit among you, just as I have among other Gentile peoples. To Greeks and barbarians, wise and foolish, I have my obligations. So for my part, I am eager to preach the gospel to you who are in Rome as well. For I am not ashamed of the gospel. It is a divine power bringing salvation to everyone who believes, to the Jew first and then to the Greek. For it brings a revelation of God's justice through faith and to faith, as the Scripture says: 'He who is just through faith shall live.' *(Rom 1:8-17)*

God's Message to Mary

In the sixth month, the angel Gabriel was sent from God to a town in Galilee called Nazareth, to a virgin betrothed to a man named Joseph, who was of the house of David. Her name was Mary. Gabriel went into her home and said to her: 'Hail, full of grace! The Lord is with thee.' Mary was much troubled by his words and wondered what this manner of greeting might mean. But the angel said to her: 'Have no fear, Mary; thou hast found grace with God. Behold thou shalt conceive in thy womb and bear a son, and thou shalt name him Jesus. He will be great, and will be called the Son of the Most High; and the Lord God will give him the throne of his forefather David; he will rule over the house of Jacob for ever, and his kingdom will have no end.'

Mary said to the angel: 'How will this be, for—am I not to know man?' The angel answered: 'The Holy Spirit will come upon thee, and the power of the Most High will overshadow thee. And therefore the holy child to be born of thee will be called God's Son. And behold, thy cousin Elizabeth too has conceived a son, old as she is; she who is believed to be barren, is now in her sixth month, for with God nothing will prove impossible.' Then Mary said: 'Behold the handmaid of the Lord! Be it done to me according to thy word.' And the angel left her.

In those days, Mary set out and went eagerly to Zachary's home in the hill-country of Judah. She went in and greeted Elizabeth; and when Elizabeth heard her greeting, the babe leaped in her womb. Elizabeth was filled with the Holy Spirit and cried aloud: 'Blessed art thou among women, and blessed is the fruit of thy womb! Who am I that the mother of my Lord should come to me? Behold, when thy greeting sounded in my ears, the babe in my womb leaped for joy. Blessed art thou for thy faith that the Lord's message will be fulfilled!' And Mary said: 'My soul gives glory to the Lord, and my spirit rejoices in God my Saviour. He has looked on the lowliness of his handmaid, and from this day forth all generations will call me blessed!' (*Lk 1:26-48*)

Reflection

In the first half of this gospel, God creates a new life within the womb of Mary at the word of the angel Gabriel: 'The Lord is with thee.' God effects what the word signifies, and the Lord is with Mary, conceived of the Holy Spirit in her virginal womb. In the second half of the passage, God quickens the life of John within the womb of his mother Elizabeth through the word of Mary. There is reason to suspect that perhaps originally it was Mary who said to Elizabeth: 'Blessed art thou among women, and blessed is the fruit of thy womb';[1] and it was perhaps Elizabeth, not Mary, who sang the Magnificat, thanking God for removing her 'lowliness' or childlessness (cf. 1 Sam 1:11). If the greeting belongs originally to Mary, she said 'Blessed art thou among women,' and Elizabeth was filled with the Holy Spirit; she added 'and blessed is the fruit of thy womb,' and John leaped for joy.

We have here two demonstrations of the power of God's word, spoken by his envoy, to effect what it signifies. First, the word is spoken by the angel, then it is spoken by Mary, and in both cases it is effective. In each case,

---

[1] The words were true of Elizabeth, but the evangelist has seen that they are still more true of Mary.

because it is accepted with faith, it produces life and more abundant life, and the recipient rejoices. By way of contrast, in the annunciation to Zachary, because the angel's word was met with disbelief, it caused a lessening of life —in the dumbness of Zachary—and sadness and shame when he was unable to complete his ministry by pronouncing the priestly blessing upon the people.

In the passage from Romans, St Paul is extolling the power of God's word, spoken by his apostles and missionaries. If he can visit the Romans, his spoken word will impart to them some spiritual gift and strengthen them, for the gospel which he preaches is the instrument or vehicle of God's power, bringing salvation to those who believe.

It is not everyone who can speak in God's name, but only those whom he has 'sent'. To Zachary the angel said: 'I am Gabriel, and I have been sent (*apestalên*) to bring you this good news,' and Mary was (by implication) sent to Elizabeth when the angel told her of Elizabeth's pregnancy. The archangel Gabriel is the first apostle, and Mary is the second. At the other end of the gospel, too, an angel is the first apostle of the resurrection, and the second is another Mary—Mary Magdalene.

Let us renew our faith in the efficacy of the blessings which God imparts to us through his envoys. Such blessings are vehicles of grace if accepted with faith. From the court of heaven may the Blessed Virgin pronounce her blessing upon us!

At the same time let us take warning. The incident at the beginning of the Infancy narratives can be profitably compared with the slaughter of the Holy Innocents at the end. Zachary's inability to bless the people of Jerusalem is a sign and symbol of the failure of the old temple-worship to keep the people in God's peace, with his blessing resting upon them. The slaughter of the Innocents was a portent and a warning of what was to befall in A.D. 70, when the wrath of God fell on Jerusalem and not a stone was left upon a stone. Jesus blessed his disciples as he ascended into heaven, but he did not pronounce a blessing on the whole people of Jerusalem. In the crisis of the war of 66-70, the Christians, warned by a revelation, fled to Pella beyond the Jordan and were saved. The rest who stayed behind in the old Jerusalem perished miserably by starvation, the sword, and crucifixion.

The world no longer believes that peace depends upon God's blessing and that war is God's scourge. The unbeliever will say: 'If a word of blessing is effective, why does not the Pope stop wars by pronouncing his blessing?' The answer is in St Matthew, chapter 10 (v. 13): if a blessing is pronounced upon the unworthy, it will return to its sender; it will remain only upon the worthy.

Prayer

Look down with favour, O Lord God our Father, upon your people, and raise up in our midst holy priests to speak words of blessing and forgiveness. Our hearts are ready to receive them with faith. Fill us all with the joy of salvation! Preserve all men from sin and all nations from collective greed, for the sake of the innocents who must otherwise suffer. Show us, O Lord, how we can care for the poorer nations. We confess that we have sinned collectively by omission in this matter. Bless our rulers with wisdom and generosity. Through our Lord Jesus Christ your Son, who lives and reigns with you in the unity of the Holy Spirit, and is God, world without end. Amen.

3

The Lord is with you

God's Message to Gideon

Now the angel of the Lord came and sat under the oak at Ophrah, which belonged to Joash the Abiezrite, as his son Gideon was beating out wheat in the wine press, to hide it from the Midianites. And the angel of the Lord appeared to him and said to him, 'The Lord is with you, you mighty man of valour.' And Gideon said to him, 'Pray, sir, if the Lord is with us, why then has all this befallen us? And where are all his wonderful deeds which our fathers recounted to us, saying, "Did not the Lord bring us up from Egypt?" But now the Lord has cast us off, and given us into the hand of Midian.' And the Lord turned to him and said, 'Go in this might of yours and deliver Israel from the hand of Midian; do not I send you?' And he said to him, 'Pray, Lord, how can I deliver Israel? Behold, my clan is the weakest in Manasseh, and I am the least in my family.' *(Jud 6:11-16)*

God's Message to Mary

In the sixth month, the angel Gabriel was sent from God to a town in Galilee called Nazareth, to a virgin betrothed to a man named Joseph, who was of the house of David. Her name was Mary. Gabriel went into her home and said to her: 'Hail, full of grace! The Lord is with thee.' Mary was much troubled by his words and wondered what this manner of greeting might mean. But the angel said to her: 'Have no fear, Mary; thou hast found grace with God. Behold thou shalt conceive in thy womb and bear a son, and thou shalt name him Jesus. He will be great and will be called the Son of the Most High; and the Lord God will give him the throne of his forefather David; he will rule over the house of Jacob for ever, and his kingdom will have no end.' Mary said to the Angel: 'How will this be, for—am I not to know man?' The angel answered: 'The Holy Spirit will come upon thee, and the power of the Most High will overshadow thee. And therefore the holy child to be born of thee will be called God's Son. And behold, thy cousin Elizabeth too has conceived a son, old as she is; she who is believed to be barren is now in her sixth month, for with God nothing will prove impossible.' Then Mary said: 'Behold the handmaid of the Lord! Be it done to me according to thy word.' And the angel left her. (*Lk 1:26-38*)

Reflection

When the angel said to Gideon 'The Lord is with thee,' Gideon did not suppose that the word was addressed to himself alone. He replied, frankly and rather boldly: 'Pray, sir, if the Lord is with us, why has all this befallen us?' — Why are we living in fear of the Midianites and Amalekites? Mary might have replied to Gabriel in the same way, for Jerusalem was ruled by a vassal of the Romans.

But Mary was more docile than Gideon. She believed that God was again drawing near to his people to deliver them—as Zachary said in the Benedictus: 'Blessed be the Lord God of Israel, for he has looked graciously upon his people and brought them deliverance. As he promised through the lips of his ancient prophets, he has raised for us a beacon of salvation in the house of his servant David, to save us from our enemies and from the power of all who hate us.' For a long time, it had seemed that God had abandoned his people and disowned his covenant. For centuries there had not been a single prophet. Now at last God draws near again, but not to a mighty man of valour. This time he comes to a virgin in a village called Nazareth. 'Rejoice,' says the angel—and the joy is not for Mary alone; God has come to dwell permanently among his people, to be with them always, giving fresh life, and hope, and joy.

He did not come to deliver the Jews from the yoke of Roman imperialism. Christ did not throw in his lot with the 'Zealots' or freedom-fighters of his day. He came to liberate his believing disciples from their spiritual enemies, the devil, the world, and the flesh, so that they might walk before him in the ways of peace, and learn to love one another as brothers, rich and poor, slave and free, Jew and Gentile, white and coloured.

Mary is the first Ark of the Covenant, for the divine presence lodges first in her. But God has come to lodge in the hearts of all who are reborn of water and the Holy Spirit. Every Christian is like a woman with child, in that he carries the divine Child within him. If he treats his Guest with reverence, he, like Mary, can utter powerful words of blessing. Even those who, like Elizabeth, have long believed themselves sterile, will find that they are not —if only they will believe, for 'nothing is impossible to God.'

Prayer

O Lord God of Israel, too long have we sat desolate like a widow. Let your Holy Spirit overshadow us, and let Christ your Son be born in us anew. We are your servants and the sons of your Handmaid! Grant that we may always live under the shadow of your wing.

4

The ark of the covenant

David welcomes the Ark

David arose and went with all the people who were with him to Baalejudah, to bring up from there the ark of God, which is called by the name of the Lord of hosts who sits enthroned on the cherubim. And they carried the ark of God upon a new cart, and brought it out of the house of Abinadab which was on the hill; and Uzzah and Ahio, the sons of Abinadab, were driving the new cart with the ark of God; and Ahio went before the ark. And David and all the house of Israel were making merry before the Lord with all their might, with songs and lyres and harps and tambourines and castanets and cymbals.

And when they came to the threshing floor of Nacon, Uzzah put out his hand to the ark of God and took hold of it, for the oxen stumbled. And the anger of the Lord was kindled against Uzzah; and God smote him there because he put forth his hand to the ark; and he died there beside the ark of God. And David was angry because the Lord had broken forth upon Uzzah; and that place is called Perezuzzah to this day. And David was afraid of the Lord that day; and he said, 'How can the ark of the Lord come to me?' So David was not willing to take the ark of the Lord into the city of David; but David took it aside to the house of Obededom the Gittite. And the ark of the Lord remained in the house of Obededom the Gittite three months; and the Lord blessed Obededom and all his household.

And it was told King David, 'The Lord has blessed the household of Obededom and all that belongs to him, because of the ark of God.' So David went and brought up the ark of God from the house of Obededom to the city of David with rejoicing; and when those who bore the ark of the Lord had gone six paces, he sacrificed an ox and a fatling. And David danced before the Lord with all his might; and David was girded with a linen ephod. So David and all the house of Israel brought up the ark of the Lord with shouting, and with the sound of the horn.

(*2 Sam 6:2-15*)

Elizabeth welcomes Mary

In those days, Mary set out and went eagerly to Zachary's home in the hill-country of Judah. She went in and greeted Elizabeth; and when Elizabeth heard her greeting, the babe leaped in her womb. Elizabeth was filled with the Holy Spirit and cried aloud: 'Blessed art thou among women, and blessed is the fruit of thy womb! Who am I that the mother of my Lord should come to me? Behold, when thy greeting sounded in my ears, the babe in my womb leaped for joy. Blessed art thou for thy faith that the Lord's message will be fulfilled!' And Mary said: 'My soul gives glory to the Lord, and my spirit rejoices in God my Saviour. He has looked on the lowliness of his handmaid, and from this day forth all generations will call me blessed. He who is mighty has done great things for me (holy is his name!). His mercy abides from generation to generation over those who fear him. He puts forth his arm in power, and scatters men who glory in their heart's conceit. He throws down monarchs from their thrones, but raises up the lowly. He loads the hungry with good things, but sends the wealthy from him empty. He has come to the aid of his servant Israel, and remembered, as he promised to our fathers, the mercy which he pledged to Abraham and to his issue for ever.' Mary stayed with Elizabeth about three months, and then returned home. (*Lk 1:39-56*)

Reflection

The ark of the covenant was a gilded chest of acacia wood in which the Israelites preserved the tablets of the Law given at the making of the covenant on Sinai. The chest had a lid or cover of solid gold, upon which were two golden cherubim; and the glory of God was believed to rest like a cloud upon these cherubim. The ark was brought up to Jerusalem by David, and when his son Solomon built the first temple, it was housed in the Holy of Holies. Its place, therefore, was at the very heart of the Jewish religion. When Jerusalem was captured by Nebuchadnezzar in 587, the ark of the covenant disappeared. The Holy of Holies of the second temple, built at the instigation of Haggai and Zechariah in 536-516, and that of Herod's temple, begun in 20 B.C., were empty. When Zachary received his annunciation in the temple, there was no ark of the covenant in Jerusalem.

At the Annunciation to Mary, God created a new Ark of the Covenant in the person of Mary. In the words of the angel, 'the power of the Most High came to overshadow her'—to rest upon her, as formerly upon the golden cherubim. In the narrative of the Visitation, the evangelist shows that he recognises Mary as the new Ark of the Covenant by inserting at least two reminiscences of the narrative from the Second Book of Samuel. David at first shrank from taking the ark into Jerusalem, and said: 'How can the ark of the Lord come to me?' and Elizabeth protests: 'Who am I that the mother of my Lord should come to me?' And just as 'the ark of the Lord remained in the house of Obededom the Gittite three months; and the Lord blessed Obededom and all his household,' so too Mary remained three months and brought a blessing upon Elizabeth and John. Perhaps too the leaping of John and the loud cries of his mother are meant to remind us of the dancing and shouting which accompanied the arrival of the old ark into Jerusalem.

These allusions show us that veneration for Mary goes back to the very beginnings of the Church—to the very earliest stratum of the gospel tradition. Later theologians have thought of many fine titles for Mary, but none is more awe-inspiring than this: that Mary is the new and true Ark of the Covenant. Just as Jesus has many titles which can be arranged in ascending order: he is prophet, prince, Messiah, king, priest, Lord, Son of Man, Son of God; so too Mary has a litany of titles. The highest is 'Mother of God', but 'Ark of the Covenant' is not far behind. Perhaps St Joseph was the first to look upon Mary in this way; and perhaps, in God's providence, the fate of Uzzah was for the instruction of Joseph.

The title 'Ark of the Covenant' belonged to Mary chiefly but not only during her pregnancy, while Christ was within her. The angel did not say: 'The child to be born of you will be the Son of God, and therefore the power of the Most High will overshadow you,' but the other way round. There is no reason to think that when Jesus was born, the glory departed from his mother. She remained the Ark of the Covenant—and shares this honour with all who are united by faith to the Body of her Son. All had sinned and all were deprived of the glory of God; but all who believe are forgiven, and the glory is restored.

Prayer

Father almighty, would that we had eyes to see the glory of the Blessed Virgin and of all the saints, both in heaven and on earth! Inspire us with reverence for your presence in ourselves and in our neighbours; and may we never drive the glory away by sinful conduct. *Foederis arca, ora pro nobis!*

5

The new name

Elijah under the Broom Tree

Ahab told Jezebel all that Elijah had done, and how he had slain all the prophets with the sword. Then Jezebel sent a messenger to Elijah, saying, 'So may the gods do to me, and more also, if I do not make your life as the life of one of them by this time tomorrow.' Then he was afraid, and he arose and went for his life, and came to Beersheba, which belongs to Judah, and left his servant there.

But he himself went a day's journey into the wilderness, and came and sat down under a broom tree; and he asked that he might die, saying, 'It is enough; now, O Lord, take away my life; for I am no better than my fathers.' And he lay down and slept under a broom tree; and behold, an angel touched him, and said to him, 'Arise and eat.' And he looked, and behold, there was at his head a cake baked on hot stones and a jar of water. And he ate and drank, and lay down again. And the angel of the Lord came again a second time, and touched him, and said, 'Arise and eat, else the journey will be too great for you.'

And he arose, and ate and drank, and went in the strength of that food forty days and forty nights to Horeb the mount of God. *(1 Kgs 19:1-8)*

The Naming of John

The time came for Elizabeth's delivery, and she gave birth to a son. When her neighbours and relatives heard of the great mercy which the Lord had shown her, they joined in her rejoicing; and on the eighth day, when they came for the child's circumcision, they wanted him called Zachary, after his father. But his mother said: 'No, he is to be named John.' 'But,' they said, 'there is no one among thy kinsfolk who bears that name.' Then they asked his father, by signs, what he wished him to be called. He asked for a writing-tablet and, to the wonder of all, wrote down 'John is his name.' At once his mouth was opened and his tongue was loosed, and he began to speak and to bless God. The neighbours were all struck with awe, and these events became the talk of the whole hill-country of Judaea. All who heard of them laid them up in their hearts, wondering what was the destiny of the child. For the hand of the Lord was with him. *(Lk 1:57-66)*

Reflection

A puzzling feature of the the story of the naming of St John is what caused the astonishment of his kinsfolk. Zachary was deaf and dumb, but he could write. He had received a divine command, brought to him by the angel Gabriel in the temple, that the child was to be called 'John'. Surely during the nine months of his dumbness and of Elizabeth's pregnancy he must have written down for her an account of what happened in the temple, and must have told her that the child was to be called John. Some of the best commentators will not admit this. It is said, for example, that 'the story loses all point if we imagine that Elizabeth and Zachary had arranged the matter previously.'[1] Hence it is conjectured that Elizabeth received the name John by a special divine inspiration, and that what caused astonishment was that Zachary who could not hear what she was saying should nevertheless want the same name. This makes it a very naive tale.

But if we suppose that Zachary had written an account of his vision for Elizabeth, what happened was this: when the kinsfolk came for the circumcision, Elizabeth said that the child was to be called 'John' and that this was Zachary's wish. The kinsfolk objected on the ground that no one in the family had the name 'John'; and they could not believe that an old conservative like Zachary would depart from custom in this way. So they appealed to Zachary, and he replied in writing: '*John* is the boy's name.' The first thing that caused astonishment was the departure from tradition, and the second, which enhanced their emotion, was that God confirmed the choice of name by removing Zachary's deafness.

The text nowhere explains the particular significance of the name 'John', which means 'Yah(weh) has favoured', or something of the kind. It does not sum up the whole mission of the Baptist, as 'Jesus' sums up the office of our Saviour. Why, then, did God insist on this name? The answer appears to be: simply because it was a departure from tradition. The choice of a new name, not borne by his father or (what was commoner) by his grandfather, nor by any of his uncles, was an omen of John's life. He came from priestly stock, but he was not to follow in the traditions of his family; he was to turn his back on the temple and its sacrifices, and go and make a new start in the desert, baptizing with water. God gave new names both to John and to Jesus because through them he was making a new beginning; neither of them was to take over the

---

[1] J. M. Creed, *The Holy Gospel according to St Luke,* ad loc.

name and the way of life of any of his ancestors. God wished to produce a new breed, who would worship him in spirit and truth, a race of men who would turn out better than their fathers. To mark the new beginning, he chose new names.

In some religious orders and congregations, it has hitherto been the custom to give new names to novices, to impress on them that they are beginning their lives over again. But unfortunately the mere name does not carry with it the character or wisdom of its former bearers. If we are to turn out better than our fathers, it cannot be done simply by changing names. God must do it— through the heavenly bread which he bids us rise and eat.

Prayer

We appeal to you, our heavenly Father, to restore the youth and vigour of your Church. Let us not grow old, or weary, or complacent, or discontented. Intervene again, O Lord, and make us better than our fathers, or our life will become tedious, and our witness ineffectual. Fill us with the spirit, not of wine or strong liquor, but of Elijah, of John, and of our Lord Jesus Christ, your Son, who lives and reigns with you in the unity of the Holy Spirit, and is God, world without end. Amen.

Note: Chronologically, the Annunciation to Joseph belongs here. It is not recorded by St Luke, but only by St Matthew. See below, pp.5-53.

6
The two censuses

David enrolls the People

Again the anger of the Lord was kindled against Israel, and he incited David against them, saying, 'Go, number Israel and Judah.' So the king said to Joab and the commanders of the army, who were with him, 'Go through all the tribes of Israel, from Dan to Beersheba, and number the people, that I may know the number of the people.' But Joab said to the king, 'May the Lord your God add to the people a hundred times as many as they are, while the eyes of my lord the king still see it; but why does my lord the king delight in this thing?' But the king's word prevailed against Joab and the commanders of the army. So Joab and the commanders of the army went out from the presence of the king to number the people of Israel...

When they had gone through all the land, they came to Jerusalem at the end of nine months and twenty days. And Joab gave the sum of the numbering of the people to the king; in Israel there were eight hundred thousand valiant men who drew the sword, and the men of Judah were five hundred thousand.

But David's heart smote him after he had numbered the people. And David said to the Lord, 'I have sinned greatly in what I have done. But now, O Lord, I pray thee, take away the iniquity of thy servant; for I have done very foolishly.' (*2 Sam 24:1-4,9-10*)

Augustus enrolls the People

In those days, an edict went out from Caesar Augustus for a census to be taken of the whole world. (This census took place before Cyrinus was governor of Syria). The people all went to be enrolled, each in his own city; and Joseph, who belonged to the house and family of David, went up from the city of Nazareth in Galilee, to be enrolled in the city of David called Bethlehem in Judaea. With him went Mary his espoused wife, who was with child. While they were there, her time came, and she brought forth her first-born son; and she wrapped him in swaddling-clothes, and laid him in a manger, because there was no room for them at the inn. (*Lk 2:1-7*)

Reflection

The evangelist sees a remarkable coincidence in that Christ our Lord came into the world to enroll citizens for his kingdom at the very time when the Roman emperor was beginning to take a complete census of his subjects. Chiefly for taxation purposes, Augustus instituted a policy of compiling lists of the men in each province and region, and of their property. St Luke says that this policy embraced 'the whole inhabited world' (in Greek, *oikoumenê*[1])—which, strictly speaking should include not only Roman provinces like Syria, but also client kingdoms like Judaea. Since the client kingdoms were nominally independent, Augustus could not *order* a census in Judaea; but it is likely enough

---

[1] The word 'ecumenical' is derived from *oikoumenê*.

that Herod decided to fall in with the emperor's policy and conduct a census in Judaea. It would both please the emperor and make his own tax-collecting more efficient.

St Luke could, then, have said that the census was ordered by Herod, but he preferred to attach it to the name of Augustus, partly because Herod was acting in pursuance of the policy of Augustus, and partly in order to emphasize the universality of the census. At the time when the whole world was being enrolled by the Roman emperor, God sent forth his Son to enroll all men into the kingdom of heaven.

St Luke also mentions a Roman governor named Cyrinus or Quirinius. Most scholars think he has committed a chronological blunder in doing so, for Quirinius became governor of Syria in A.D. 6, and Jesus cannot have been born as late as A.D. 6 if he was about thirty years old in A.D. 29. The best solution to this problem is, I think, the one adopted by Lagrange: the sentence should be translated (as above): '*This* census took place *before* Cyrinus was governor of Syria'—it is a chronological 'footnote' incorporated into the text by the evangelist,[1] to explain that the census during which Jesus was born was *not* the main census which provoked the revolt of the Zealots in A.D. 6 (when the Romans took over direct control of Judaea). The purpose of the note is to clear up a possible confusion, to show that Jesus was born in a time of peace, and perhaps also to create a link with the Passion narrative, where another 'Cyrenius' (Simon of Cyrene) appears—and is enrolled with his two sons in the kingdom of God.

St Luke, then, draws a comparison between two censuses. But perhaps he also wishes to draw a contrast. He may have shared the view embodied in the Book of Samuel that the taking of a census by a human ruler was an act of pride and a usurpation of the rights of God. Among the

[1] There were no footnotes in ancient books.

Jews this feeling was still strong in the time of Quirinius. The leader of the Zealot revolt condemned the census as an instrument of tyranny: the Galileans would soon find themselves in a condition of 'downright slavery,' he said. (Perhaps one use made of the census-list compiled at the time of Christ's birth was the extermination of the male children of the house of David from two years and under.) It is quite possible, therefore, that in the evangelist's mind the Roman census was an instrument of enslavement, carried out by the emperor's servants, whereas the enrolment begun by Jesus was an instrument of liberation, carried out by God's Son, in order to grant sonship and freedom to the enrolled. At Bethlehem, Mary brough forth her Son, the First-Born (*prôtotokon*)—the firstborn of many brethren.

Nowadays we no longer feel that a government acts sinfully when it carries out a census, but we can still contemplate with wonder the providential coincidence to which St Luke draws our attention; and we can thank God that 'our names are written on the citizen-rolls of heaven.' St Luke is the only evangelist who records the saying of Christ in which this phrase occurs (cf. Lk 10:17-20).

Prayer

We give thee thanks, almighty Father, for enrolling us in the Book of Life. May thy kingdom be extended wider still and wider, for the salvation of all races and nations throughout the inhabited world. May all who are baptized already be reunited in one Church. May we show ourselves worthy of our citizenship, and always find strength in our hope of an inheritance in thy heavenly kingdom. Through our Lord Jesus Christ, thy Son, who lives and reigns with thee in the unity of the Holy Spirit, and is God, world without end. Amen.

7
No room at the inn

Death outside the City

Jesus, when he wished to sanctify the people by his own blood, suffered outside the city gate. So then let us go to him outside the camp, bearing his disgrace. For here on earth we have no abiding city; we are making our way to the city that is to come. *(Heb 13:12-14)*

Birth outside the City

While they were there, her time came, and she brought forth her first-born son; and she wrapped him in swaddling-clothes, and laid him in a manger, because there was no room for them at the inn. *(Lk 2:6-7)*

Reflection

St Luke's brief allusion to the rejection of Joseph and Mary at Bethlehem is very surprising. The thing itself is surprising enough: that Joseph's relations in Bethlehem did not exert themselves to make Mary welcome and comfortable for the birth of her child. And St Luke's way of narrating it is surprising too—the barest facts, without comment.

A possible explanation comes to light if one considers the question: where was Joseph living at the time of the Annunciation to Mary? The answer can hardly be: At Nazareth, because then Mary would have told him at once what the angel had said to her and why she was going off into Judaea to visit Elizabeth; and at least after the angel's prophecy about Elizabeth had been verified, Joseph would surely have believed. If in these circumstances he had refused to believe, he would have been more blameworthy than Zachary. So Joseph must have lived elsewhere. He probably learned of Mary's pregnancy through a third party and without hearing of the angel's prophecy about Elizabeth and its fulfilment.

Where, then, was Joseph living? The possible answers can be divided into two: either at Bethlehem, or elsewhere —perhaps at Sephoris or at Tiberias, where there were large building projects. If he was not at Bethlehem, he would feel no difficulty about taking Mary there for the census, since the people of Bethlehem would not know the date of his marriage and could not take scandal over Mary's advanced pregnancy. But if he was at Bethlehem at the time when the angel appeared to him and bade him take Mary his wife, the people of Bethlehem knew the date of his marriage; and if he returned within three or four months with his wife in an advanced state of pregnancy, they would suspect adultery. Under such circumstances, Joseph would not take her to Bethlehem unless forced to do so; but perhaps he was forced to, by the census (unfortunately we do not know the census requirements). If so, we have an explanation of how the Child came to be laid in a manger: Joseph's relations were inhospitable to Mary and unpleasant to Joseph because they believed Mary to be an adultress; and the explanation of St Luke's brevity and obscurity is that he does not wish to say this so plainly.

If this conjecture is correct, the hostility and rejection which brought Jesus to his death were already prefigured at his birth. He was born, too, outside the city, bearing shame. And the whole scene is invested with great pathos: Mary knows herself to be the mother of God, and at the same time she is rejected as an adultress; she undergoes a self-emptying to match her Son's, who, being in the form of God, took the form of a slave. This gives fresh point to the visit of the shepherds and the appearance of the angels. Mary needed such consolation.

This is a scene to remember, when one is wrongly judged by others. God did not spare Jesus, Mary and Joseph. Some saints have even had the courage to *want* to go through this kind of experience, in order to become like Jesus and Mary and Joseph.

Prayer

With the example of Jesus and Mary and Joseph before me, O heavenly Father, may I not be afraid of men's disapproval, so long as I have your approval and grace. When temptations come upon me, teach me to remain at peace and not to rebel, but to find my consolation in you. Through our Lord Jesus Christ your Son, who lives and reigns with you in the unity of the Holy Spirit, and is God, world without end. Amen.

8
The Lamb of God

A Lamb is Lost

Jesus told them this parable: 'If any of you has a hundred sheep and loses one of them, does he not leave the ninety-nine in the desert and go after the lost sheep until he finds it? And when he finds it, does he not put it on his shoulders joyfully, and come home and call his friends and neighbours together and say to them, "Rejoice with me, because I have found the sheep that I had lost"? I tell you, in the same way there will be rejoicing in heaven over one sinner who repents rather than over ninety-nine just men who have no need of repentance.' (*Lk 15:3-7*)

A Lamb is Found

She brought forth her first-born son; and she wrapped him in swaddling-clothes, and laid him in a manger, because there was no room for them at the inn.

In that same country there were shepherds out in the open, keeping the night-watches over their flocks; and behold, an angel of the Lord stood by them, and the glory of the Lord shone about them, and great fear came upon them. But the angel said to them: 'Have no fear! For behold, I bring you good tidings of great joy for all the people. A Saviour has been born for you this night, in the city of David. He is the Lord Messiah. The sign by which you will know him is this: you will find a babe wrapped in swaddling-clothes and laid in a manger.' Then suddenly there appeared with the angel a great throng of the heavenly army praising God and singing: 'Glory to God on high, and on earth peace to men in whom he is well-pleased.'

When the angels left them and went back into heaven, the shepherds said to one another: 'Come then, let us go over to Bethlehem and see this new thing which the Lord has made known to us.' They went with all haste and found Mary and Joseph, and with them the babe laid in a manger. When they had seen him, they made known what had been told them about the child. (*Lk 2:7-17*)

Reflection

The story of the shepherds at the Nativity bears interesting resemblances to several later scenes in the gospels. The shepherds become the first disciples. Like Peter and Andrew, James and John, they are at their daily work when God's call comes to them, and they leave their work to go after Jesus. They leave the ninety-nine sheep on the mountain side to go and look for the Lamb of God, who lies, fittingly, in a manger. When they find him, they are filled with joy and tell their neighbours, and their joy is a visible image of the joy of the angels in heaven.

The scene is also like the burial and resurrection of Jesus. The Son of Man, having no place of his own to lay his head, is born in another man's stable and buried in another man's grave. In each scene there is a Mary and a Joseph—at Bethlehem his parents, at the tomb Mary Magdalene and Joseph of Arimathea. The one Joseph provides swaddling-clothes in which he is wound round and round; the other provides the winding cloth for his burial. When Peter and John run to the tomb, the winding-sheet is their sign—they see it and believe; when the shepherds go to the stable, the swaddling-clothes are the sign which enables them to believe. The angel's short-term prophecy, that they would find a child wrapped in swaddling-clothes and laid in a manger, had proved true; therefore they believed his long-term gospel, that is, his announcement that the Child was their Saviour. We can also infer that the salutary act of faith, which brings peace to men of God's good pleasure, and with this peace the joy of salvation, can be made by one who is contemplating the crib—not only by one who is contemplating the cross.

The reason for the joy of the angels and for the praise which they offer to God is not simply the metaphysical wonder of the Incarnation—the assumption of our human nature into unity of person with the Godhead; they are also rejoicing in God's goodness to men in sending a Saviour to grant peace and reconciliation to believers. The first recipients of this peace and reconciliation are the shepherds, for they believe in Jesus as their Saviour. They know very little about the historical Jesus—indeed so far there is very little to know—but already they are capable of believing and of receiving the graces offered to believers.

The scene also resembles another event in which Peter, James and John took part—the Transfiguration. To judge from St Luke's account, the Transfiguration took place by night (cf. Lk 9:37). The disciples first saw the glorious vision and were struck with fear: then the glory departed, and they saw 'only Jesus'. So too here: the scene of glory occurs outside, and when it is over they see just a babe lying in a manger—'only Jesus'. Both scenes reveal how Christ emptied himself in becoming a man. He became like us, shorn of the glory of God, in order that we might become like him.

May he renew in us the joyful faith of the shepherds, and grant us that peace which is his Father's glory. For God is glorified when we are contented and bless him for his gifts.

Prayer

Lord Jesus, once a babe in swaddling-clothes and now seated at the right hand of the Father, I firmly believe that you will save me; renew in me the joy of salvation, so that I may render thanks to God the Father for ever, for his greater glory. Amen.

9

The Saviour is born

Salvation from Sickness and Death

As soon as Jesus crossed back in the boat to the other side, a great crowd gathered to meet him. He was still on the shore, when a president of one of the synagogues came to him. Jairus was his name. He fell at Jesus' feet when he saw him, and earnestly begged his help: 'My little daughter is at the point of death,' he said; 'come and lay your hands on her, and you will save her life.' So Jesus went away with him, accompanied by great crowds which pressed about him.

Now there was a woman who had suffered from haemorrhages for twelve years, and had endured much at the hands of many doctors, and spent all she had without becoming any the better, but rather worse. As she had heard about Jesus, she came up behind him in the crowd and touched his cloak, thinking to herself: 'If I touch even his clothes, I shall be healed.' At once the source of the haemorrhages was dried up, and she felt in her body that she was cured of her complaint. Jesus knew at once that power had gone out from him, and he turned round in the crowd and said: 'Who touched my clothes?' His disciples said: 'With the crowds as you see pressing round you, how can you ask, "Who touched me?"' Jesus was looking round to see who had done it. But the woman, who was in fear and trembling because she knew what had happened to her, came and fell at his feet and told him the whole truth. He said to her: 'Daughter, your faith has cured you. Go in peace, and you will remain free from your complaint.'

While he was still speaking, a message came from the house of the president of the synagogue: 'Your daughter is dead; why trouble the Master any more?' But Jesus overheard the message and said to the president: 'Do not be afraid; only have faith!' He allowed no one to accompany him except Peter and James and John the brother of James. When they reached the president's house, he found a noisy crowd of people wailing and lamenting loudly. So, as he went in, he said to them: 'What is the reason for this noise and lamentation? The child is not dead, she is only asleep.' They laughed at him; but after he had sent them all away, he took the child's father and mother and his own companions, and went into the room where the child lay. He took her by the hand and said to her: '*Talitha, koum,*' which means: 'Little girl, (I bid you) rise up!' At once the girl rose up and began to walk about (she was twelve years old), and the people were beside themselves with amazement. Jesus strictly charged them that no one was to know of it, and he told them to give her something to eat. (*Mk 5:21-43*)

The Saviour of His People

In that same country there were shepherds out in the open, keeping the night-watches over their flocks; and behold, an angel of the Lord stood by them, and the glory of the Lord shone about them, and great fear came upon them. But the angel said to them: 'Have no fear! For behold, I bring you good tidings of great joy for all the people. A Saviour has been born for you this night, in the city of David. He is the Lord Messiah. The sign by which you will know him is this: you will find a babe wrapped in swaddling-clothes and laid in a manger.' Then suddenly there appeared with the angel a great throng of the heavenly army praising God and singing: 'Glory be to God on high, and on earth peace to men in whom he is well-pleased.'

When the angels left them and went back into heaven, the shepherds said to one another: 'Come then, let us go over to Bethlehem and see this new thing which the Lord has made known to us.' They went with all haste and found Mary and Joseph, and with them the babe laid in a manger. When they had seen him, they made known what had been told them about the child; and all who heard were filled with wonder at what the shepherds told them.

(*Lk 2:8-18*)

Reflection

As we saw, there are some remarkable resemblances between the stable or cave at Bethlehem and the cave in which Jesus was buried. The narrative of the Raising of Jairus's Daughter comes between, and forms a link between the birth of Jesus and his burial. As at Bethlehem, there are three persons, the father, the mother, and the child, not exactly in a cave, but in an inner room off a courtyard; but as at the sepulchre, the child is dead. Outside in the courtyard is a noisy crowd of mourners weeping and lamenting over the death of the child; they correspond, by way of contrast, to the multitudes of angels at Bethlehem praising God for the birth of the Child Jesus. Then, as at the sepulchre, God wakes up the child from the sleep of death. The name 'Jair' means 'God awakens.'

Theologically, the scenes are linked by the concepts of salvation and resurrection. The angel at Bethlehem told the shepherds that 'a Saviour has been born.' The shepherds may have thought this meant a new king to replace the Herods. It is gradually revealed in the course of the gospel in what sense Jesus is our Saviour: he saves us from sin and all the consequences of sin, including death. In raising Jairus's daughter, Christ our Lord reveals himself as the one who has power to save from the last enemy, Death. His work as Saviour will not be complete until at the Last Day he transforms our risen bodies into the likeness of the body which he has in his glory (cf. Phil 3:21).

The other scene too, the Cure of an ailing Woman, which is enclosed in the Raising of Jairus's Daughter, can be usefully compared with the nativity at Bethlehem. In both incidents, Jesus is in the midst of a crowd—at Bethlehem there is the crowd of people who have come for the census. And in both cases Jesus is, as it were, unknown to the crowd: at Bethlehem there is no room for him in their houses, and in the Cure of the Woman with Haemorrhages only the one woman has faith enough to draw on his power —many are jostling him on all sides, but she alone touches him with faith. She recognises him as a Saviour, for she says: 'If I touch but the hem of his garment, I shall be *saved*.' It is curious that there is mention of Jesus's garments here—as at Bethlehem, at the sepulchre, and at the Transfiguration.

Further, just as the shepherds are struck with fear at the sudden revelation of angels in the heavens, so this woman is struck with fear when the power of Christ is revealed in curing her. She comes 'fearing and trembling' to acknowledge her theft of a miracle. Then Jesus tells her to 'go in peace', just as the angels announced peace to the shepherds.

Christ is still secretly present in the world; he is God in our midst, and therefore, as St Paul says, we should serve him 'in fear and trembling' (Phil 2:12). If we touch but the hem of his garments with faith in our touch, we shall be saved from our sin, and from weakness, and ultimately from death.

Prayer

O Lord Jesus Christ, source of life and holiness, grant us health of body and soul, and make us always duly grateful for these gifts. Who livest and reignest with God the Father in the unity of the Holy Spirit, world without end. Amen.

10
The heavenly liturgy

Angels and Saints

You have drawn near to Mount Sion and the city of the living God, the heavenly Jerusalem, where the countless hosts of angels dwell and the assembly of the first-born whose names are inscribed in heaven; there too is God, the Judge of all; there are the spirits of the just who have attained their end; there is Jesus, the Mediator of the New Covenant, whose cleansing blood cries louder than the blood of Abel.

(Heb 12:22-24)

Angels and Shepherds

Then suddenly there appeared with the angel a great throng of the heavenly army praising God and singing: 'Glory to God on high, and on earth peace to men in whom he is well pleased.' When the angels left them and went back into heaven, the shepherds said to one another:

'Come then, let us go over to Bethlehem and see this new thing which the Lord has made known to us.'

(*Lk 2:13-15*)

Reflection

The shepherds at Bethlehem were given a brief glimpse of the heavenly liturgy—of the multitudinous host of heaven praising God and crying: 'Glory to God in the highest.' The early Church attached far greater importance to these angels, and to all angels, than we do. We regard them as adding much to the beauty of the story, but hardly as being anything real. Yet the angels are real. Christ our Lord spoke of the angels in the same way as he spoke of demons —implying quite clearly that they are real. St Paul too had no doubt about them; and the Apocalypse is full of them.

One of the sources of our difficulties over the angels is that they appear in the infancy narratives and after the resurrection, but not during the public ministry—which makes some people suspect that the beginning and end of the gospel story have been overlaid with mythological elements, whereas the public ministry has not. But there is a good reason for the absence of the angels during the public ministry: when the Lord is present, preaching the gospel (cf. Heb 2:3), he himself acts—in person, and not through angels. One of the marks of the superiority of the New Testament over the Old is that in the New, God deals *directly* with men. Angels appear in the infancy narratives because Jesus is not yet able to speak for himself, and in the resurrection narratives they appear only when he is absent. They should be taken seriously. They are a reminder that the universe is more mysterious than we commonly think. God is the creator of all things visible and invisible; and, as the author of Hebrews says (11:3), men of faith believe that the visible proceeds from the invisible. If the whole visible world were to pass away, there would still be a vast invisible creation of angels praising God and crying 'Glory to God in the highest.'

As we know from the Dead Sea Scrolls, the monks at Qumran were anxious to ensure that their own liturgy was in unison with the heavenly liturgy of the angels. One of the reasons why they did not take part in the liturgy of the temple at Jerusalem was that they believed the priesthood of the temple to be following a calendar different from that followed by the angels in heaven and therefore to be celebrating the great feasts on the wrong days. This kind of reasoning sounds very crude, but it springs from a sound religious instinct—the wish to join human worship to the worship of God's other servants, the angels.

When the temple at Jerusalem became obsolete, the new temple, the Body of Christ, the home of the Shekinah, became the centre of a new, heavenly Jerusalem—which for a time was on this earth. Then Christ our Lord ascended into heaven, and his heavenly court and his angels became the new Jerusalem. His disciples on earth looked up to the new Jerusalem as the centre of their cult. They were on the fringe, but truly united to it, for wherever two or three are gathered in Christ's name, he is spiritually present to them and therefore they to him. The liturgy is still full of expressions of the desire to unite human worship to angelic. We should do well to take these more seriously.

In the early Church, the life of a monk, especially, was understood as the attempt to live an angelic life, keeping watch by night and by day, unceasingly singing God's praise. The shepherds at Bethlehem can be regarded as the prototypes of Christian monks, in so far as they were keeping watch by night when they were admitted to share in the heavenly liturgy. The spirituality of monasticism held out the hope of becoming more and more like the angels, whose nature is not to be *and* to be able to sing God's praise, but rather whose very nature it is to be singing God's praise. The monk hopes to become an organ in which the wind of the Holy Spirit will make music for the praise of God, almost independently of his own conscious will and activity. But as St Paul spoke of such things when writing to the Roman church at large (cf. Rom 8:26), this ambition is not for monks alone.

Prayer

Grant, O heavenly Father, that the ancient ideal of angelic purity may not be forgotten among your people here on earth. Grant that we may all come closer to living such a life; and grant that you Holy Spirit may descend upon some of the monks and nuns of our day with gifts of charismatic prayer. Through Jesus Christ, your Son, our Lord, who lives and reigns with you in the unity of the same Holy Spirit, and is God, world without end. Amen.

11
The new Rachel

Joseph's Prophetic Dream

Now Joseph had a dream, and when he told it to his brothers they only hated him the more. He said to them, 'Hear this dream which I have dreamed: behold, we were binding sheaves in the field, and lo, my sheaf arose and stood upright; and behold, your sheaves gathered round it, and bowed down to my sheaf.' His brothers said to him, 'Are you indeed to reign over us? Or are you indeed to have dominion over us?' So they hated him yet more for his dreams and for his words. Then he dreamed another dream, and told it to his brothers, and said, 'Behold, I have dreamed another dream; and behold, the sun, the moon, and eleven stars were bowing down to me.' But when he told it to his father and to his brothers, his father rebuked him, and said to him, 'What is this dream that you have dreamed? Shall I and your mother and your brothers indeed come to bow ourselves to the ground before you?' And his brothers were jealous of him, but his father kept the saying in mind. (*Gen 37:5-11*)

Joseph's Dream Fulfilled

They went with all haste and found Mary and Joseph, and with them the babe laid in a manger. When they had seen him, they made known what had been told them about the child. But Mary treasured all these things, pondering them in her heart. The shepherds went away giving glory and praise to God for all they had seen and heard; for they had found everything exactly as had been revealed to them. (*Lk 2:16-17,19-20*)

Reflection

The sentence about Mary's 'pondering' is reminiscent of two passages in the Old Testament. After Joseph has described his dreams, the text ends: 'his father kept the word.' And secondly, at the end of the great vision of the Son of Man in Daniel, chapter 7, the prophet says: 'As for me, Daniel, my thoughts greatly alarmed me, and my colour changed, but I kept the matter in my mind.' The words in St Luke which we translate 'pondering them' (*sumballousa*) probably mean 'comparing them'. So the meaning may well be that Mary preserved the memory of the visit of the shepherds and compared it with passages in the Old Testament read out in the liturgy, and with later events in the life of Jesus. If so, Mary's meditations were typological comparisons.

What resemblances did she see between the visit of the shepherds and Joseph's dreams in Genesis, chapter 37? When Joseph narrates the dream of the sheaves to his brothers, they ask: 'Are you indeed to lord it over us?'—which has a parallel in the angel's announcement that Jesus is to be the Lord Messiah or the Anointed Lord. Then Joseph tells his father the dream of the sun and the moon and the eleven stars bowing down to him, and his father asks: 'Shall I and your mother and brothers indeed come to bow down to the ground before you?' And at Bethlehem the shepherds, who are Jesus' brothers in the sense that they too belong to the house of David and to David's city of Bethlehem, come and bow down with Mary and Joseph before Jesus. The text does not explicitly say that they bowed down, but the Magi did, and the shepherds came for the same purpose as the Magi. The parallel is the stronger because Joseph's brothers in Genesis are shepherds.

The sentence in Daniel, chapter 7, that 'Daniel kept the matter in mind,' may be a deliberate reminiscence of Genesis, chapter 37, because the vision of Daniel 7 is of the establishment of a Jewish empire (the rule of the Son of Man) over the Gentiles, and this had been prefigured in the rule of the Jew Joseph over Egypt. If Mary saw a parallel between the nativity scene and Daniel 7, she may have considered that there in the cave was the inauguration of the fulfilment of Daniel's vision: the Son of Man, to start with, was among the beasts, as it were a guest in their domain, but soon he was to be raised up to rule over them.

It seems, then, that the patriarch Joseph prefigures the Son of Man seen by Daniel, and Daniel's Son of Man turns out to be Jesus. Joseph was the firstborn of his mother Rachel, but not of Jacob; and Jesus is the firstborn of Mary, but not of St Joseph. Therefore Mary is a new Rachel—a most fitting name, since 'rachel' means 'a ewe-lamb' or 'mother lamb' (cf. Gen 31:28), and Mary is the mother of the Lamb of God. This new Rachel preserves the memory of the nativity in silence, perhaps in conscious fulfilment of the prophecy of Isaiah (53:7): 'Like a lamb that is led to the slaughter, and like a sheep (*rachel*) that before its shearers is dumb, so he opened not his mouth.' In Mary, we have the first and greatest Christian contemplative. May she teach and inspire us to keep these things in our hearts, pondering them.

Prayer

Grant, O heavenly Father, that while we ponder these things in our hearts, after the example of the Blessed Virgin, we too may be filled with the Holy Spirit and enabled to praise your goodness, for ever and ever. Amen.

12

Nunc dimittis

Israel recognises Joseph

So Israel took his journey with all that he had, and came to Beersheba, and offered sacrifices to the God of his father Isaac. And God spoke to Israel in visions of the night, and said, 'Jacob, Jacob.' And he said, 'Here am I.' Then he said, 'I am God, the God of your father; do not be afraid to go down to Egypt; for I will there make of you a great nation. I will go down with you to Egypt, and I will also bring you up again; and Joseph's hand shall close your eyes.' Then Jacob set out from Beersheba; and the sons of Israel carried Jacob their father, their little ones, and their wives, in the wagons which Pharaoh had sent to carry him. They also took their cattle and their goods, which they had gained in the land of Canaan, and came into Egypt, Jacob and all his offspring with him, his sons, and his sons' sons with him, his daughters, and his sons' daughters; all his offspring he brought with him into Egypt... He sent Judah before him to Joseph, to appear before him in Goshen; and they came into the land of Goshen. Then Joseph made ready his chariot and went up to meet Israel his father in Goshen; and he presented himself to him, and fell on his neck, and wept on his neck a good while. Israel said to Joseph, 'Now let me die, since I have seen your face and know that you are still alive.'

(*Gen 46:1-7,28-30*)

Symeon recognises Jesus

Now there was a man in Jerusalem named Symeon, a just and devout man, who lived in hope of the consolation of Israel, and the Holy Spirit was upon him. He had received a revelation from the Holy Spirit that he would not see death until he had seen the Lord's Anointed. He came in the Spirit into the temple; and when the parents brought in the child Jesus, to carry out the custom of the Law for him, Symeon took him into his arms and blessed God with these words: 'Now thou dost dismiss thy servant, O Lord, in peace, for thy promise is fulfilled. For my eyes have seen the salvation which thou has ordained for all the nations to behold: a light of revelation for the Gentiles, and of glory for thy people Israel.' (*Lk 2:25-32*)

Reflection

When Jesus is brought into the temple, Symeon greets him with paternal affection, as if he were a long-lost child. His last great wish has been fulfilled; now he can depart this life in peace. So he sings his *Nunc dimittis*, a sigh of relief and gratitude—'Now, O Lord, thou dost dismiss thy servant according to thy word in peace.'

It is a beautiful scene, and yet a little puzzling. What advantage was there for him in seeing the beginning of Christ's life and not surviving to see its completion? Why did he attach so much importance to *seeing* the Child? After all, a new-born baby is very uncommunicative.

There is an incident in the life of one of our Forty Martyrs which is of some assistance here: Philip Howard,

Earl of Arundel, was imprisoned for the faith by Elizabeth I. Shortly after his imprisonment, his wife gave birth to a child. But for a long time the Queen would not allow the prisoner to be told whether it was a boy or a girl. Even after he had found out that it was a boy, his son and heir, he was not allowed to see the boy. He was kept for twelve years in the Tower of London before he was finally executed. When his execution was near, he was tortured with longing to see his son before he died, and sent a most pitiful petition to the Queen—which she refused. He died without seeing the boy. It is not difficult to sympathize with his longing; we can easily guess what he felt. In his case too one might say: 'Of what advantage would it have been to *see* his son, if he must die soon after?' And the answer is: Clearly a great advantage—a very precious moment of love in the contemplation of his son and heir, and then the precious memory to carry with him to his death.

Symeon's longing for the Messiah was, I suppose, something like that. He wanted hope to give place to vision and love before he died. All he saw was a little child, wrapped from chin to feet in swaddling clothes, and yet it was enough. He saw him and loved him. The tension of unfulfilled hope was resolved, his heart was soothed and pacified by love. And with the eyes of faith his prophetic mind saw much more than the tiny face.

But perhaps the Biblical example of Jacob and Joseph is more enlightening. It is a moment of restoration and reconciliation; Jacob's family is reunited after half a lifetime of division. Jacob has not dared to hope or pray for it; he believed his son was dead. But Symeon had wrestled in prayer throughout his life; now God has returned to his people, Symeon's wrestling is over, his service is complete, he can die in peace. This world can hold no greater joy for him. He has seen the best of his days at the very end.

As for us, we have not seen our Lord with our bodily eyes, but we have the advantage of living in the better half of human history, *after* the coming of the Messiah, after the completion of the work of redemption. We too have received the Holy Spirit; and when we contemplate the Child whom Mary carried into the temple, we too can greet him with love, and rejoice in our reconciliation with God. And at the end of our days, we too can hope for a consoling sign of God's presence and love, in our Last Anointing.

Prayer

Grant, O Lord, that I may die at peace with you, after completing the task which you have given me to do. And grant that some of those now living may see the day when all who call upon the name of Jesus in this our beloved land which you have given us may be reunited in one undivided Church. Through the same Jesus Christ your Son our Lord, who lives and reigns with you in the unity of the Holy Spirit, and is God, world without end. Amen.

13

The end of the Law

As under the Law

The heir, as long as he is a child, is no better than a slave, though he is the lord of all; he is under guardians and trustees until the date set by the father. So with us: when we were children, we were slaves to the elemental spirits of the universe. But when the time had fully come, God sent forth his Son, born of a woman, born under the Law, to redeem those who were under the Law, so that we might receive the adoption of sons. (*Gal 4:1-5*)

Yet not under the Law

Mary treasured all these memories, and pondered them in her heart. The shepherds went away giving glory and praise to God for all they had seen and heard; for they had found everything exactly as had been revealed to them.

The eighth day came, the day for his circumcision, and he was named Jesus, the name which the angel had called him before he was conceived in the womb.

When their days of purification had been completed as laid down in the Law of Moses, they brought Jesus up to Jerusalem to present him to the Lord, for it is decreed in the Law of the Lord that every male opening the womb shall be sacred to the Lord; they wished also to make the offering laid down in the Law of the Lord: a pair of turtle-doves or two young pigeons.

Now there was a man in Jerusalem named Symeon, a just and devout man, who lived in hope of the consolation of Israel, and the Holy Spirit was upon him. He had received a revelation from the Holy Spirit that he would not see death until he had seen the Lord's Anointed. He came in the Spirit into the temple; and when the parents brought in the child Jesus, to carry out the custom of the Law for him, Symeon took him into his arms and blessed God with these words: 'Now thou dost dismiss thy servant, O Lord, in peace, for thy promise is fulfilled. For my eyes have seen the salvation which thou hast ordained for all the nations to behold: a light of revelation for the Gentiles, and of glory for thy people Israel.' Then, while his father and mother were wondering over what was being said about Jesus, Symeon blessed them and said to Mary his mother: 'Behold, this child is destined for the fall of many and for the rise of many in Israel; he will be the object of wonder and dispute and through him the secret thoughts of many will be revealed. Yes, and your own heart too will be pierced by a sword.' (*Lk 2:19-35*)

Reflection

The narrative of how Mary and Joseph observed the requirements of the Law of Moses at the Circumcision and Presentation is not told for its own sake, to set before Jewish Christians a model of strict observance. It is part of the introductory half of the passage, setting the scene for Symeon's prophecy. Only when one has understood the point of this rather obscure prophecy is it possible to understand the introductory narrative.

What, then, does Symeon foretell? He says that Jesus lies (like a stone) for the overthrow of many and for the raising of many in Israel; that he is to be 'a sign of contradiction'—a figure who will challenge opposition—in order that the thoughts of many hearts may be revealed; and that a sword will pass even through Mary's heart.

The image of the stone or rock which either trips men up or gives them something firm to stand on is used by Isaiah in speaking of the Law. Here it is used by Symeon of Christ: he will prove a stumbling-block to many, who will reject him; but to those who believe in him he will become a rock of security. He was to become a stumbling-block to many chiefly on account of his attitude to the Law. He claimed that the Son of Man is superior to the Law and may set it aside whenever charity requires. Many who were sure that God had spoken to them through Moses were not sure that God could be speaking to them through one who seemed to break the Law; they preferred the security of the Law to the risk (as they saw it) of faith in Christ. It was chiefly on account of the Law that Jesus became a 'sign of contradiction', a subject of debate, some declaring themselves for him and some against him, and all revealing the thoughts of their hearts in the process.

The obscure prophecy about Mary, that a sword would pass through her heart, may also have reference to the Law. The sword is the symbol of division. Mary was a pious, Law-observing Jewess. When she saw her Son showing what many thought a reprehensible independence of the Law, she must have been torn between her loyalty to the Law of Moses and her unshakable belief in her Son. This sense of being torn in two directions must have been at its most acute on Calvary, for Mary doubtless knew the text of Deuteronomy (21:23): 'Cursed is every man who hangs upon a tree.' Could she believe the Law and believe no less in her Son?

St Luke says that Mary and Joseph 'wondered' over Symeon's words. They had no idea how the prophecy would be fulfilled. The introductory narrative helps us to understand both the prophecy and their wonder. Because they were simple, Law-observing Jews, their Son, who was to live under the Law without really being subject to it, was to become a puzzle, a source of anguish to them. They came into the temple piously to offer their pair of doves; at the outset of his ministry he enters the temple and creates a disturbance by driving out the sellers of doves and sacrificial animals.

It is sad to find that even in the holy family itself the older generation did not fully understand the younger. But perhaps we can find some consolation in the thought that Mary was called upon to fulfil her role in God's plans without fully understanding them, and therefore with some anguish. The same is true of most of us.

The Presentation is one of the 'joyful mysteries' of the Rosary; but each of the joyful mysteries is tinged with sorrow. If we look at the whole panorama of our Lady's life, it contained much disappointment, suffering and sadness. Through many sufferings she was led to the kingdom, advancing from faith to faith as she went. The future was disclosed to her stage by stage. As she journeyed on, the horizon moved forward. At the beginning of her history is the great and glorious promise of the Annunciation: 'You shall bear a Son... he shall be great... the Lord God will give him the throne of David, and he shall rule in the house of Jacob for ever.' But soon came the anguish of Joseph's doubts, the birth in a stable, the flight into Egypt; then Symeon's obscure prophecy, to be fulfilled on Calvary; then, after Pentecost, the anguish of the delayed return of Jesus, and of the continued refusal of Israel to believe in the gospel.

The Church is the extension of the household of Jesus and Mary: we are his brothers and her children, and we must not expect the pattern of our lives to be so very different from theirs. Our faith and our obedience will be put to the test of time, the test of disappointment, the test of suffering, and the test of incomprehension. We must not expect to stride triumphantly through this world into the next. Through many sufferings we must enter the kingdom, but these will not embitter us, if we are given the humble faith of the Blessed Virgin.

Prayer

Heavenly Father, would that I could have the faith and patience of Mary the Mother of Jesus when the sword of incomprehension pierces my heart! Sustain my hope, and give me the humility to fulfil my role, even when I cannot understand its purpose. Through the same Jesus Christ your Son our Lord, who lives and reigns with you in the unity of the Holy Spirit, and is God, world without end. Amen.

14

The end of the Temple

The Ark in the Temple of Dagon

When the Philistines captured the ark of God, they carried it from Ebenezer to Ashdod; then the Philistines took the ark of God and brought it into the house of Dagon and set it up beside Dagon. And when the people of Ashdod rose early the next day, behold, Dagon had fallen face downward on the ground before the ark of the Lord. So they took Dagon and put him back in his place. But when they rose early on the next morning, behold, Dagon had fallen face downward on the ground before the ark of the Lord, and the head of Dagon and both his hands were lying cut off upon the threshold; only the trunk of Dagon was left to him. This is why the priests of Dagon and all who enter the house of Dagon do not tread on the threshold of Dagon in Ashdod to this day. (*1 Sam 5:1-5*)

The Ark in the Temple of Jerusalem

When their days of purification had been completed as laid down in the Law of Moses, they brought Jesus up to

Jerusalem to present him to the Lord, for it is decreed in the Law of the Lord that every male opening the womb shall be sacred to the Lord; they wished also to make the offering laid down in the Law of the Lord: a pair of turtle-doves or two young pigeons.

Now there was a man in Jerusalem named Symeon, a just and devout man, who lived in hope of the consolation of Israel, and the Holy Spirit was upon him. He had received a revelation from the Holy Spirit that he would not see death until he had seen the Lord's Anointed. He came in the Spirit into the temple; and when the parents brought in the child Jesus, to carry out the custom of the Law for him, Symeon took him into his arms and blessed God with these words: 'Now thou dost dismiss thy servant, O Lord, in peace, for thy promise is fulfilled. For my eyes have seen the salvation which thou hast ordained for all nations to behold: a light of revelation for the Gentiles, and of glory for thy people Israel.' Then, while his father and mother were wondering over what was being said about Jesus, Symeon blessed them and said to Mary his mother: 'Behold, this child is destined for the fall and for the rise of many in Israel; he will be the object of wonder and dispute, and through him the secret thoughts of many will be revealed. Yes, and your own heart too will be pierced by a sword.' (*Lk 2:22-35*)

Reflection

We talk of the 'Presentation' of Jesus in the temple, as if every Jewish firstborn son went through a ceremony of 'presentation'. But in fact 'presentation' is a Christian term. There is no law in the Pentateuch which tells parents to 'present' their firstborn son before the Lord at the temple. What the Law says is that every male opening the womb, both of man and of beast, is to be *consecrated* to the Lord (Exod 13:2). This is probably a relic of a primitive stage of religion in which the firstborn was actually sacrificed to the cult-god. The expanded form of the same law given in the Book of Numbers (18:15-16) adds that the firstborn of man shall be redeemed, that is 'bought back', from the Lord for five shekels, but the firstborn of a cow or a sheep or goat may not be redeemed—it belongs to the Lord, is to be offered in sacrifice, and eaten by the priests of the temple.

In Jewish terminology, therefore, we should expect to be told by the evangelist that Mary and Joseph took the Child to the temple to 'offer' him to the Lord and to 'redeem' him. St Luke mentions the two doves offered for Mary's purification, but says nothing about the payment of the five-shekel ransom. Perhaps the reason is that Mary and Joseph were too poor to pay this sum and therefore Jesus remained unredeemed—consecrated to God as the Lamb of God ready for sacrifice. In the text of St Luke, he comes from the manger to the temple. Even before the prophecy of Symeon, therefore, there is a hint in this narrative that Jesus will one day offer his life in sacrifice.

The verb 'to present' (*parastêsai*, used transitively) is rare in the Bible. The first time it occurs is in the passage from 1 Sam 5, where we are told that the Philistines took the ark of the Covenant and 'presented' it, or made it stand (*parestêsan auten*) before Dagon in his temple. There is a remarkable resemblance between the Presentation and this scene. At the Presentation, the true Ark of the Covenant, Jesus in whom the Godhead is bodily present, enters the temple at Jerusalem. It does not fall down the next day, like the statue of Dagon; but it is already obsolete, and 'what is obsolete and growing old is ready to vanish away' (Heb 8:13). The day is at hand when neither on Mount Sion nor on Mount Gerizim will men worship the Lord, but anywhere and everywhere, in the Church, which is the Body of Christ.

If St Luke intended to insinuate the comparison between

the temple of Dagon and the temple in Jerusalem, he did not hold the temple at Jerusalem in such veneration as commentators usually say he did. On the contrary, he agreed with St Stephen. God does not dwell in temples made with hands; we are to seek him, not in splendid material rites, but in the humble service of our fellow men. If Christ identifies himself with them, they are the Ark of the Covenant.

Prayer

Grant, O Lord Jesus, that I may find thee in the midst of my fellow men, and let my service of them be a liturgy rendered to thee. Who livest and reignest with God the Father in the unity of the Holy Spirit for ever and ever. Amen.

15

Awaiting the Consolation of Israel

Words of Comfort

Comfort, comfort my people, says your God. Speak tenderly to Jerusalem, and cry to her that her warfare is ended, that her iniquity is pardoned, that she has received from the Lord's hand double for all her sins.

A voice cries: 'In the wilderness prepare the way of the Lord, make straight in the desert a highway for our God. Every valley shall be lifted up, and every mountain and hill be made low; the uneven ground shall become level, and the rough places a plain. And the glory of the Lord shall be revealed, and all flesh shall see it together, for the mouth of the Lord has spoken.'

A voice says, 'Cry!' And I said, 'What shall I cry?' All flesh is grass, and all its beauty is like the flower of the field. The grass withers, the flower fades, when the breath of the Lord blows upon it; surely the people is grass. The grass withers, the flower fades; but the word of our God will stand for ever. *(Isa 40:1-8)*

Words of Gratitude

There was a man in Jerusalem named Symeon, a just and devout man, who lived in hope of the consolation of Israel, and the Holy Spirit was upon him. He had received a revelation from the Holy Spirit that he would not see death until he had seen the Lord's Anointed. He came in Spirit into the temple; and when the parents brought in the child Jesus, to carry out the custom of the Law for him, Symeon took him into his arms and blessed God with these words: 'Now thou dost dismiss thy servant, O Lord, in peace, for thy promise is fulfilled. For my eyes have seen the salvation which thou hast ordained for all the nations to behold: a light of revelation for the Gentiles, and of glory for thy people Israel.' Then, while his father and mother were wondering over what was being said about Jesus, Symeon blessed them and said to Mary his mother: 'Behold, this child is destined for the fall of many and for the rise of many in Israel; he will be the object of wonder and of dispute, and through him the secret thoughts of many will be revealed. Yes, and your own heart too will be pierced by a sword.'

There was also a prophetess, Anna daughter of Phanuel, of the tribe of Asher, a woman far advanced in years, who had lived with her husband seven years from her maidenhood, then alone as a widow for as much as eighty-four. She was never away from the temple, but worshipped there night and day with fasting and prayers. She came at this very time, and stood beside them, and she too in turn gave thanks to God and spoke of the child to all who were living in hope of the redemption of Jerusalem.
(Lk 2:25-38)

Reflection

Symeon is described as awaiting 'the consolation of Israel', and Anna speaks about Jesus to all who are awaiting 'the redemption of Jerusalem'. The phrases imply that Israel has been in a state of desolation and bondage. The whole Presentation narrative sounds like a tacit commentary on the passage of Isaiah. God is now speaking tenderly to Israel, not in words, but in the gift of a tiny child—telling Israel that her 'humiliation' is at end and her sin redeemed. By implication Israel is compared to a sinful woman whose sin has been punished by the penalties of slavery and childlessness. Now her sin has been forgiven, the humiliation of childlessness—of being not-loved—is taken away. The Lord has given her a child who is to be the glory of Israel and the firstborn of many brethren. Henceforth all nations will look to this Child, and therefore to the Jews, for salvation. The Child himself was to say later that 'salvation is from the Jews' (Jn 4:22).

The long desolation of Israel is personified in Anna. There was a time, in her youth, when she lived for seven years with her husband; but then followed eleven times seven years of widowhood and childlessness in which she no longer enjoyed the favour of her Lord. Throughout this long period, some in Israel always continued to hope in the Lord, to trust in his fidelity, and to pray for the consolation of Israel. At length in the fulness of time, after twelve times seven years (a round number of round numbers), God is returning to offer reconciliation, restoration, and consolation to Israel. All flesh is grass, the generations come and go, the grass withers, the flower fades, but the word of God stands for ever. His fidelity is wonderful. And yet in a way more wonderful, because closer to us, is the fidelity which he inspired in the saints of the Old Testament, so that they never lost heart, but continued to serve with prayer and fasting night and day until it should please the Lord to speak tenderly to Jerusalem.

The vision of prophets is usually foreshortened. Probably both Symeon and Anna thought that the lifetime of Jesus would see a dramatic change for the better in the fortunes of Israel. But again God took his time. The gospel of St John ends, as the gospel of St Luke begins, with an old man looking forward to the consolation of Israel —when Christ returns. We are heirs of his expectation. The time which has passed since the first coming of Christ is about the same as that which elapsed between the promise to Abraham and its fulfilment. We too, like Symeon and Anna, are awaiting the consolation of Israel. They are our grandparents, we their grandchildren, and as often happens these alternate generations are close together. May we serve the Lord with as much fidelity as they did, while we sigh 'How long, O Lord, how long?'

Prayer

Heavenly Father, Creator of heaven and earth, a thousand years are as a day before you. But not before us! Have pity on the brevity of our lives, and grant us consolation before we die. Forgive us our sins, and reveal to us the joy of our salvation!

16

Wrestling with God

The Prayer of David

And the Lord struck the child that Uriah's wife bore to David, and it became sick. David therefore besought God for the child; and David fasted and went in and lay all night upon the ground. And the elders of his house stood beside him, to raise him from the ground; but he would not, nor did he eat food with them. On the seventh day the child died. And the servants of David feared to tell him that the child was dead; for they said, 'Behold, while the child was yet alive, we spoke to him, and he did not listen to us; how then can we say to him the child is dead? He may do himself some harm.' But when David saw that his servants were whispering together, David perceived that the child was dead; and David said to his servants, 'Is the child dead?' They said, 'He is dead.' Then David arose from the earth, and washed, and anointed himself, and changed his clothes; and he went into the house of the Lord, and worshipped; he then went to his own house; and when he asked, they set food before him, and he ate.

Then his servants said to him, 'What is this thing that you have done? You fasted and wept for the child while it was alive; but when the child died, you arose and ate food.' He said, 'While the child was still alive, I fasted and wept; for I said, "Who knows whether the Lord will be gracious to me, that the child may live?" But now he is dead; why should I fast? Can I bring him back again? I shall go to him, but he will not return to me.' (*2 Sam 12:15-23*)

The Prayer of Symeon and Anna

Symeon took the child into his arms, and blessed God with these words: 'Now thou dost dismiss thy servant, O Lord, in peace, for thy promise is fulfilled. For my eyes have seen the salvation which thou hast ordained for all the nations to behold: a light of revelation for the Gentiles, and of glory for thy people Israel'...

There was also a prophetess, Anna daughter of Phanuel, of the tribe of Asher, a woman far advanced in years, who had lived with her husband for seven years from her maidenhood, then alone as a widow for as much as eighty-four. She was never away from the temple, but worshipped there night and day with fasting and prayers. She came at this very time, and stood beside them, and she too in turn gave thanks to God and spoke of the child to all who were living in hope of the redemption of Jerusalem.

(*Lk 2:28-32,36-38*)

Reflection

We are probably meant to learn from this gospel that God hastened the coming of Christ in response to the prayers of pious Jews like Symeon and Anna who prayed earnestly and with almost incredible perseverance for the consolation of Israel. We can gather the nature of their petition by turning their prayers of thanksgiving back into prayers of petition:

> O Lord God of Israel,
>   look graciously upon us and redeem your people;
> raise up for us a horn of salvation
>   in the house of your servant David,
> as you promised through the lips of your prophets...
>
> When, O Lord, will you dismiss your servant,
>   according to your word, in peace?
> When shall my eyes see your salvation,
>   which you have prepared before all the people?

The prayer of Symeon and Anna was not simply a quest for conformity with the will of God—an ever-repeated petition to know his will and do it: 'Thy will be done!' Theirs was not the prayer of resignation, but of struggle: 'Thy kingdom come, quickly, in our day!' They tried, as it were, to force the hand of God—to make him act sooner than he would have done if they had held their peace. At Cana, Jesus first refused Mary's request on the ground that his hour had not yet come; then, recognising that in response to Mary's faith and petition the hour *had* come, he revealed his glory (cf. Jn 2:11). The chief servant asked, more wisely than he knew, why God had kept the good wine of the gospel until then; but the demons knew that Jesus had come 'before time' to torment them (cf. Mt 8:29).

God showed his approval of Symeon's insistent prayer by revealing to him that he would not die before he had seen the Messiah. The divine rulership of the world is not an absolute autocracy in which all movement proceeds downwards from his infinite wisdom through his higher to his lower creatures. He has given to man a mind and a will and made him capable of forming strong desires under the impulse of the Spirit. He wills that we should voice our longings in prayer, so that he, the Almighty and All-wise, may respond to them in his government of the universe. The relationship of every superior to his subject should conform to this pattern: as in the heavenly bodies, there should be interaction between the higher and the lower.

Christ himself taught us first to pray 'Thy kingdom come!' and then 'Thy will be done!' We must first say what *we* want, and then acknowledge that, in the end, if what we want does not fit into the plans of God's providence, we are content that his holy will be done. David wrestled with God for the life of his illegitimate child, so long as there was hope; but when God took the child, he went into the temple and worshipped. We too must be ready to pray with the faith and wisdom of Job: 'The Lord has given, the Lord has taken away. Blessed be the name of the Lord!'

Prayer

O Lord, you know my secret desire. If it is your will, bring it about; if it is not your will, let it become your will! In the plans of an all-wise ruler, is there not room for adjustment, and even for favouritism? O Lord, hear my prayer, so that I may know that you care for me as a person, and do not just move me about as a pawn on your chessboard.

17

Anna and Mary

The Desolation of the Daughter of Sion

How lonely sits the city that was full of people! How like a widow has she become, she that was great among the nations! She that was a princess among the cities has become a vassal. She weeps bitterly in the night, tears on her cheeks; among all her lovers she has none to comfort her; all her friends have dealt treacherously with her, they have become her enemies... But thou, O Lord, dost reign for ever; thy throne endures to all generations. Why dost thou forget us for ever, why dost thou so long forsake us? Restore us to thyself, O Lord, that we may be restored! Renew our days as of old! Or hast thou utterly rejected us? Art thou exceedingly angry with us?

(Lam 1:1-2; 5:19-22)

The Consolation of the Daughter of Phanuel

The was a prophetess, Anna daughter of Phanuel, of the tribe of Asher, a woman far advanced in years, who had lived with her husband seven years from her maidenhood, then alone as a widow for as much as eighty-four. She was never away from the temple, but worshipped there night and day with fasting and prayers. She came at this very time, and stood beside them, and she too in turn gave thanks to God:

Blessed be the Lord God of Israel, for he has looked graciously upon his people and brought them deliverance. As he promised through the lips of his ancient prophets, he has raised for us a beacon of salvation in the house of his servant David, to save us from our enemies, and from the power of all who hate us, to prove his fidelity to our fathers, his mindfulness of the holy covenant, of the oath which he swore to our father Abraham, to deliver us from the hand of our enemies, and give us power to serve him without fear, and live in holiness and justice before him all the days of our lives. *(Lk 2:36-38; 1:68-75)*

Reflection

Anna is described as 'the daughter of Phanuel' and 'of the tribe of Asher'. The evangelist must have seen some special significance in these details, or he would not have recorded them—he does not give this kind of information about Symeon. 'Asher' is Hebrew for 'blessed', and 'Phanuel' (Peniel) is explained by Jacob in Gen 32:30 as meaning 'I have seen God face to face.' So no doubt the evangelist means that Anna's personal and tribal names were omens of her destiny—to see the face of God in Jesus. But this is not all. The context in Genesis (32:24-32) describes how Jacob wrestled all night with an angel, and in the morning he 'called the name of the place Peniel, saying, "For I have seen God face to face, and my soul has been saved".'[1] Both Anna and Symeon have wrestled with God

---

[1] This translation follows the Septuagint (the ancient Greek translation of the Bible). The RSV translation, which follows the Hebrew text, is slightly different.

in prayer during a long dark night of the soul, and now at the dawn of a new era they have seen the face of God, and their souls have been saved.

The gospel text seems to imply that Anna's long widowhood was voluntary—that she refrained from entering another marriage, in order to wrestle more effectively with God.[1] Her widowhood can be understood, in the same way as her long fasts, as a kind of hunger-strike, to move the Lord to compassion so that he will come and console Israel. In order to make herself more effectively the mouthpiece of Israel, she acts the part of Jerusalem as described by Jeremiah: 'How lonely sits the city that was full of people! How like a widow she has become, she that was great among the nations!'

In the Presentation, God yields to her long prayer and comes to comfort her and Jerusalem. The encounter was an occasion of consolation and peace and grace. The Law of Moses allowed the High Priest to go into the Holy of Holies only once in the year to look upon the propitiatory or 'mercy-seat' which covered the Ark of the Covenant. At the Presentation, Anna and Symeon were allowed to look upon the true Ark of the Covenant. They saw, not just the golden mercy-seat, but the loving-kindness of God revealed in flesh and blood in the Child Jesus. For them it was the Day of Atonement, of reconciliation, of peace. Symeon sang his *Nunc dimittis;* Anna sang her canticle —probably the first half of the *Benedictus* really belongs to her—and then she went away to serve God in holiness and justice all the remaining days of her life. They looked upon the little Child, and what did they see? Very little, and yet it was effective. Here perhaps we have a justification of the rite of Benediction, in which the Eucharist is not eaten but looked upon: at Benediction we are a priestly people looking upon the ark of the covenant and the mercy-seat of God.

[1] Cf. 1 Cor 7:5 and 1 Cor 7:25-35.

Mary is another Anna. She too is a prophetess, a daughter who sees God face to face, and is blessed among all women. She lived in virginal marriage with St Joseph for at least twelve years, then spent the rest of her life in widowhood. The years of her widowhood were spent more in gratitude than in wrestling with God—and yet, perhaps, in some measure Mary too wrestled and uttered the groanings of the Spirit, crying *Marana tha* ('Our Lord, come!') —for the final consolation of Israel that is still to come.

Prayer

Come, Lord Jesus, to console your people. Pour out upon us your Holy Spirit, so that we may walk before you in holiness and justice all the days of our lives. Then our guardian angels will always look upon the face of our Father in heaven.

18

Beginning, middle and end

A Woman Clothed with the Sun

Then God's temple in heaven was opened and the Ark of the Covenant was seen inside. There were flashes of lightning, rumbles and peals of thunder, an earthquake, and a great storm of hail.

Then a great sign appeared in heaven: a woman clothed in the sun, with the moon beneath her feet and a crown of twelve stars on her head. She was with child, and in the anguish of her birth-pangs cried out to be delivered of her child.

Then another sign appeared in heaven: I saw a great red dragon with seven heads and ten horns and seven diadems on its seven heads, and its tail swept down a third of the stars of heaven and cast them on the earth. Then the dragon stood before the woman who was about to give birth, so as to devour the child when she brought it forth. The child she brought forth was a male, a son, destined to rule all the nations with a rod of iron. Her child was snatched up to God and to his throne, and the woman fled into the desert, where God had prepared for her a place of refuge. There she will be cared for during twelve hundred and sixty days. (*Apoc 11:19-12:6*)

The Vision of Symeon

There was a man in Jerusalem named Symeon, a just and devout man, who lived in hope of the consolation of Israel, and the Holy Spirit was upon him. He had received a revelation from the Holy Spirit that he would not see death until he had seen the Lord's Anointed. He came in the Spirit into the temple; and when the parents brought in the child Jesus, to carry out the custom of the Law for him, Symeon took him into his arms and blessed God with these words: 'Now thou dost dismiss thy servant, O Lord, in peace, for thy promise is fulfilled. For my eyes have seen the salvation which thou hast ordained for all the nations to behold: a light of revelation for the Gentiles, and of glory for thy people Israel.' Then, while his father and mother were wondering over what was being said about Jesus, Symeon blessed them and said to Mary his mother: 'Behold, this child is destined for the fall of many and the rise of many in Israel; he will be the object of wonder and of dispute, and through him the secret thoughts of many will be revealed. Yes, and your own heart too will be pierced by a sword.' (*Lk 2:25-35*)

Reflection

The Jews saw history as a cyclic movement, in which later events follow the pattern of earlier cycles of events. They liked to describe the later events in words and phrases reminiscent of the earlier, so that the reader would recognise the hand of God at work—somewhat as one recognises the hand of a painter in his later paintings after studying his early ones. So when St John attempts to describe, in the Apocalypse, the events which will surround the second coming of Christ, he does so in phrases and images borrowed from the first coming. By examining them carefully we can see how he understood the events of the first coming—and how he saw in them a renewal of still earlier events in which God had shown his hand.

The beginning of the passage from the Apocalypse (11:19) may contain an allusion to the Presentation, for it was then that the Ark of the Covenant appeared in the temple. Mary carries in her arms the Child Jesus in whom the Shekinah has its resting-place. He is not only the Ark of the Covenant; in a sense he *is* the new covenant, the new link between God and man—not a fictitious kinship, but a real kinship within one family and one person.

The next image St John proposes is a composite one: Mary in her pregnancy, and Mary later, when the sword pierced her heart. In her pregnancy, she was the new Rachel. The sun above her and around her is God, the Father of her Child—her Child being the new Joseph. The twelve stars are the brethren of Jesus who will come to adore him, and the moon beneath her feet is her own symbol. But unlike Rachel, Mary suffers her anguish, not in childbirth, but later—at the Massacre of the Infants, the Loss of Jesus and Finding in the Temple (when she described her own pain of loss as 'birth-pangs'), and most of all on Calvary.

During her pregnancy, the devil was not allowed to touch the Ark of the Covenant, but waited 'that when she was delivered, he might devour the child.' Almost as soon as the Child was born, Satan moved Herod to attempt to devour the Child with the mouth of the sword. But the Child was saved by his parents, who fled into the desert, and to Egypt.

St John describes these events in language reminiscent of the sentences pronounced upon the woman and the serpent in Genesis. Mary is the new Eve; and in the infancy narratives she wins her first victory over the Serpent. Symeon and Anna at the Presentation are representative figures: Symeon embodies the hopes and the fidelity of Israel, and Anna's life has recapitulated its history—a brief period of marriage to Jahweh in her youth, followed by a long period of widowhood and desolation, now to end. It is probable, then, that in the Presentation narrative, as in the passage of the Apocalypse, Mary is a representative figure: she is the new Eve, mother not only of Jesus, the Son of Man, but of all the living. She personifies the new Israel, the Church, as Symeon and Anna personified the old Israel. That is why St John can go on (in v. 6) to describe the Church hiding in the desert under the image of the Woman—he is no longer speaking of Mary personally, but of the Church which she represents.

The identification of Mary as the second Eve is not just a pious idea of certain later theologians. It is an element of the earliest tradition. Here in the infancy of Jesus the history of mankind begins again. We are offered the choice: to remain sons of the old Eve, or to throw in our lot with the new Eve and the second Adam.

Prayer

Heavenly Father, grant that I may be daily reborn from on high, to become one of the twelve stars surrounding the Blessed Virgin, for the adoration of her Son and yours, who lives and reigns with you in the unity of the Holy Spirit, and is God, world without end. Amen.

Note: Chronologically, the Visit of the Magi, the Massacre of the Innocents, and the Flight into Egypt belong here. They are not recorded by St Luke, but only by St Matthew. See below, pp. 95-110.

19

A cloud of sadness

The Boy Samuel in the Temple

Now the boy Samuel was ministering to the Lord under Eli. And the word of the Lord was rare in those days; there was no frequent vision. At that time, Eli, whose eyesight had begun to grow dim, so that he could not see, was lying down in his own place; the lamp of God had not yet gone out, and Samuel was lying down within the temple of the Lord, where the ark of God was. Then the Lord called, 'Samuel! Samuel!' and he said, 'Here I am!' and ran to Eli and said, 'Here I am, for you called me.' But he said, 'I did not call; lie down again.' So he went and lay down. And the Lord called again, 'Samuel!' And Samuel arose and went to Eli and said, 'Here I am, for you called me.' But he said, 'I did not call, my son; lie down again.' Now Samuel did not yet know the Lord, and the word of the Lord had not yet been revealed to him. And the Lord called Samuel again the third time. And he arose and went to Eli, and said, 'Here I am, for you called me.' Then Eli perceived that the Lord was calling the boy. Therefore Eli said to the boy, 'Go, lie down; and if he calls you, you shall say, "Speak, Lord, for thy servant hears".' So Samuel went and lay down in his place.

And the Lord came and stood forth, calling as at other times, 'Samuel! Samuel!' And Samuel said, 'Speak, for thy servant hears.' Then the Lord said to Samuel, 'Behold, I am about to do a thing in Israel, at which the two ears of every one that hears it will tingle. On that day I will fulfil against Eli all that I have spoken concerning his house, from beginning to end. And I tell him that I am about to punish his house for ever, for the iniquity which he knew, because his sons were blaspheming God, and he did not restrain them. Therefore I swear to the house of Eli that the iniquity of Eli's house shall not be expiated by sacrifice or offering for ever.'

Samuel lay until morning; then he opened the doors of the house of the Lord. And Samuel was afraid to tell the vision to Eli. But Eli called Samuel and said, 'Samuel, my son.' And he said, 'Here I am.' And Eli said, 'What was it that he told you? Do not hide from me. May God do so to you and more also, if you hide anything from me of all that he told you.' So Samuel told him everything and hid nothing from him. And he said, 'It is the Lord; let him do what seems good to him.'

And Samuel grew, and the Lord was with him and let none of his words fall to the ground. (*1 Sam 31:19*)

The Boy Jesus in the Temple

The parents of Jesus used to go up to Jerusalem every year for the feast of the Passover. When he was twelve years old, they went up as usual for the festival; but when the feast days were over and they started back, the boy Jesus stayed behind in Jerusalem. His parents did not know of it but thought he was in the company. At the end of a day's journey they looked for him among the relatives and friends, and as they could not find him, they turned back towards Jerusalem in search of him. After three days they found him in the temple, sitting among the teachers, listening to them and asking them questions. Everyone who heard him was amazed at the intelligence which he shewed in his answers. When his parents saw him they were greatly surprised; and his mother said to him: 'My son, why have you treated us like this? Your father and I have suffered deeply while searching for you.' He said to them: 'Why did you need to search? Surely you knew that I would be in my Father's house?' But they did not understand the word that he spoke to them. Then he went down with them to Nazareth and was obedient to their authority. His mother treasured all these words in her heart; and as Jesus grew older, he advanced in wisdom and in grace with God and men. *(Lk 2:40-52)*

Reflection

It is a common complaint nowadays that parents do not understand their children, and children do not understand their parents. Looking back to the holy family at Nazareth, we might hope to find things entirely different, but alas! we do not. The failure of the older generation to understand the younger is to be observed even in the holy family —and the difficulty arises because the younger does not conform to the established uses of the older. Jesus causes pain to his parents by his assertion of independence, and when his mother asks him to explain, neither she nor Joseph can understand his reply. As we say, there was a breakdown of communication. Mary's grief remained, and a slight estrangement crept in—a lack of perfect understanding. The situation has a surprisingly modern look. We thought these troubles began only yesterday.

What is more, if this incident is considered in conjunction with the Presentation, the two scenes exemplify one of the very latest discoveries or observations of the sociologists, the 'principle of alternate generations', namely, that there is often a better understanding between grandparents and their grandchildren than between parents and their children. Symeon shows a greater understanding of Jesus than has been granted at this stage to Mary and Joseph, and he seems to foresee that the child will cause pain to his pious parents. In the Presentation-narrative, Mary and Joseph are astonished at what Symeon says, and in the Finding-narrative they are astonished at what Jesus says.

The sadness of this scene in the life of the holy family is intensified when it is compared to the narrative of the boyhood of Samuel, where there is a charming relationship between Samuel and his mother, Hannah: 'she used to make for him a little robe and take it to him each year, when she went up with her husband to offer the yearly sacrifice. Then Eli would bless Elkanah and his wife, and say: "The Lord give you children by this woman for the loan which she lent to the Lord." So then they would return home.' Samuel has the consolation of knowing that by serving the Lord he is bringing blessings upon his parents; and Hannah can look forward to the joy of seeing Samuel again and giving him a present made with her own hands. In the Lucan incident, by contrast, there is a painful lack of understanding between Jesus and his parents—and it seems so unnecessary, because surely a further attempt at explanation would have brought light and peace.

The evangelist seems to ignore these difficulties, and to expect the reader to be filled with naive wonder at the Child's precocious wisdom. But is this wisdom? One is more inclined to borrow St Augustine's famous phrase and say: *Est mysterium!* Could the meaning possibly be that Jesus wished to hint to his parents that if they thought about the matter, they would see it was God's will that he should stay and be educated in the temple—and that as they did not see it, he obeyed them and went back to Nazareth?

But on dogmatic grounds it is almost impossible to believe that throughout the Hidden Life the will of God was not done in regard to the education of his Son. Perhaps this scene contains an anticipation of Jesus' struggle in Gethsemane: at the age of twelve he feels a natural desire to stay in the temple and attend the lessons of the scribes (there can have been little opportunity for study and instruction at Nazareth, out of which no good was expected to come); and he showed his obedience by giving up his natural desire and embracing the will of his Father, mediated to him by Mary and Joseph.

It must be assumed that they thought carefully about what education they ought to give to the exceptional Child entrusted to them, and that they also considered *where* they ought to live. If an angel had told them to remove to Jerusalem, no doubt they would have obeyed as promptly as they did at the time of his birth. They must have been instructed in some way that they were to remain at Nazareth. In the light of St John, chapter 7 (14-16), we can see the providential purpose in this: it was plain to the people of Jerusalem during the public ministry that Jesus had not received his wisdom and doctrine from any human teacher: 'Half way through the festival, Jesus went up to the temple and began to teach. The Jews were shocked and said: 'How can this man know the Scriptures without having studied?' Jesus answered them: 'My teaching is not my own; it is the teaching of the one who sent me.'

Prayer

Come, O Holy Spirit, and teach us to live at peace with our elders and our youngers. Give us the gift of patience and of speech, to compose our differences and attain an appreciative understanding of one another. Enlighten us to guide and instruct the younger generation according to the will of Jesus Christ our Lord, who lives and reigns with God the Father, for ever and ever. Amen.

20

The true
Son of David

David's Kindness to Saul

When Saul returned from following the Philistines, he was told, 'Behold, David is in the wilderness of Engedi.' Then Saul took three thousand chosen men out of all Israel, and went to seek David and his men in front of the Wildgoat's Rocks. And he came to the sheepfold by the way, where there was a cave; and Saul went in to relieve himself. Now David and his men were in the innermost parts of the cave. And the men of David said to him, 'Here is the day of which the Lord said to you, "Behold, I will give your enemy into your hand, and you shall do to him as it shall seem good to you".' Then David arose and stealthily cut off the skirt of Saul's robe. And afterward David's heart smote him, because he had cut off Saul's skirt. He said to his men, 'The Lord forbid that I should do this thing to my lord, the Lord's anointed, to put forth my hand against him, seeing he is the Lord's anointed.' So David persuaded his men with these words, and did not permit them to attack Saul. And Saul rose up and left the cave, and went upon his way.

Afterwards David also arose, and went out of the cave, and called after Saul. 'My lord the king!' And when Saul looked behind him, David bowed with his face to the earth, and did obeisance. And David said to Saul, 'Why do you listen to the words of the men who say, "Behold, David seeks your hurt"? Lo, this day your eyes have seen how the Lord gave you today into my hand in the cave; and some bade me kill you, but I spared you. I said, "I will not put forth my hand against my lord; for he is the Lord's anointed." See, my father, see the skirt of your robe in my hand; if I cut off the skirt of your robe, and did not kill you, you may know and see that there is no wrong or treason in my hands. I have not sinned against you, though you hunt my life to take it. May the Lord judge between you and me, may the Lord avenge me upon you; but my hand shall not be against you. As the proverb of the ancients says, "Out of the wicked comes forth wickedness"; but my hand shall not be against you. After whom has the king of Israel come out? After whom do you pursue? After a dead dog! After a flea! May the Lord therefore be judge, and give sentence between me and you, and see to it, and plead my cause, and deliver me from your hand.'

When David had finished speaking these words to Saul, Saul said, 'Is it your voice, my son David?' And Saul lifted up his voice and wept. He said to David, 'You are more righteous than I; for you have repaid me good, whereas I have repaid you evil. And you have declared this day how you have dealt well with me, in that you did not kill me when the Lord put me into your hands. For if a man finds his enemy, will he let him go away safe? So may the Lord reward you with good for what you have done to me this day.' (*1 Sam 24:1-18*)

Joseph's Kindness to Mary

The birth of Jesus Christ came about in this way. While Mary his mother was betrothed to Joseph, before they were united in marriage, she came to be with child by the Holy Spirit. Joseph, who was to marry her, being a just man, and not wishing to expose her to shame, meant to put her away privately. He had come to this decision, when an angel of the Lord appeared to him in a dream, and said: 'Joseph, son of David, do not hesitate to take Mary to be your wife; for the child conceived by her is of the Holy Spirit. She will give birth to a son, and you shall call him Jesus, for it is he who will save his people from their sins.' (*Mt 1:18-21*)

Reflection

Some recent writers have proposed the view that St Joseph contemplated breaking off his engagement to Mary, not because her pregnancy seemed to imply misconduct, but because he knew that the Child was the Son of God and did not feel that he ought to pass himself off as the father of such a Child. This interpretation has certain attractions. The pious Christian does not like to think that St Joseph suspected Mary of adultery; and these writers point out that according to v. 18, Joseph found out, not just that Mary was pregnant, but that she was pregnant of the Holy Spirit.

But from ancient times, in fact from the time of Justin (150 A.D.) the phrase 'of the Holy Spirit' has been read as an anticipatory comment put in by the evangelist, not as a part of what St Joseph found out. The text shows that St Joseph had passed beyond the point of considering *whether* he should 'break off his engagement' (as we say) or 'divorce his wife' (as the Greek says [1]), and was con-

---

[1] The vocabulary used here in Mt 1:19-20 resembles that used in the divorce-text, Mt 5:32. The reason why St Luke omits the Annunciation to Joseph may be that he does not wish to shock his readers by suggesting that a threat of 'divorce' hung over the relationship of Mary and Joseph for however brief a time.

sidering *how* he should do it. And the main point of the angel's appearance is to inform him that the Child is of the Holy Spirit and therefore he need not fear to take Mary as his wife—he need not fear that by doing so he would offend God by condoning adultery.

Joseph is described as 'being a just man and not wishing to make an example of her.' The word 'just' is almost certainly to be understood here in the Hebrew sense of 'merciful'.[1] He wished to do what was right according to the Law, yet without applying the rigour of the Law— which in this case were extremely severe. According to the statute laid down in the Book of Deuteronomy (22:22-23), if Mary was found guilty of adultery during her betrothal, she might be punished by stoning. Under the Romans, the Jews were not allowed to inflict the death penalty according to their law; but at this time neither Judaea nor Galilee was under Roman rule. Therefore Mary was in real danger. The angel of the Annunciation had good reason to say to her: 'Do not be afraid!' and she showed great courage in saying: 'Be it done unto me according to your word!' She was placing herself in a situation in which she would need God's protection.

He saved her by sending the angel to Joseph. In his 'justice' or 'kindness' Joseph was already considering a way of saving Mary, when God revealed to him a simpler and still kinder way. It is highly appropriate that the angel should begin his message with the words: 'Joseph, son of David,' for Joseph, by his kindness, had proved himself a true son of David. He had reason to suspect that Mary had committed a grave wrong against him. Her life was in his hands; but he wished to spare her, as David spared Saul.

During his public ministry, Jesus was once called upon to pronounce judgment on a woman who not only seemed

---

[1] The 'justice' of God which is revealed in the gospel (Rom 1:16) is called in Tit 3:4 'the lovingkindess' of God.

to be guilty, but was guilty, under the law of Deuteronomy 22:23. He refused to condemn her, and treated her with touching kindness. He too was a true son of David, full of grace and truth.

If the text is understood as explained above, both Mary and Joseph went through a great trial during their betrothal. For Mary it was a trial of courage and faith in God; for Joseph it was a trial of his gentleness and kindness. They both trusted in God; and God provided, with the temptation, an issue or way out (cf. 1 Cor 10:13).

Prayer

Teach us all, O Lord Jesus, to be reluctant to judge one another, and to be kind and gentle towards those who seem to be in the wrong; for we ourselves hope to be treated with mercy on the Day of Judgment.

21
Solomon and Jesus

The Queen of Sheba

Now when the queen of Sheba heard of the fame of Solomon concerning the name of the Lord, she came to test him with hard questions. She came to Jerusalem with a very great retinue, with camels bearing spices, and very much gold, and precious stones; and when she came to Solomon, she told him all that was on her mind. And Solomon answered all her questions; there was nothing hidden from the king which he could not explain to her. And when the queen of Sheba had seen all the wisdom of Solomon, the house that he had built, the food of his table, the seating of his officials, and the attendance of his servants, their clothing, his cupbearers, and his burnt offerings which he offered at the house of the Lord, there was no more spirit in her.

And she said to the king, 'The report was true which I heard in my own land of your affairs and of your wisdom, but I did not believe the reports until I came and my own eyes had seen it; and, behold, the half was not told me; your wisdom and prosperity surpass the report which I heard. Happy are your wives! Happy are these your servants, who continually stand before you and hear your wisdom! Blessed be the Lord your God, who has delighted in you and set you on the throne of Israel! Because the Lord loved Israel for ever, he has made you king, that you may execute justice and righteousness.' Then she gave the king a hundred and twenty talents of gold, and a very great quantity of spices and precious stones; never again came such an abundance of spices as these which the queen of Sheba gave to king Solomon. (*1 Kgs 10:1-10*)

Magi from the East

After the birth of Jesus, which took place at Bethlehem in Judaea during the reign of Herod, Magi from the East arrived in Jerusalem and asked: 'Where is the new-born king of the Jews? We observed his star in the East and have come to worship him.' Hearing this, king Herod was perturbed, and with him the whole of Jerusalem. He called an assembly of all the chief priests and scribes of the people, and asked them where the Messiah would be born. They replied: 'At Bethlehem in Judaea; for so God says through the prophet in Scripture: "And you, Bethlehem in the land of Judah, are by no means least among the leaders of Judah, for out of you will come a leader, to shepherd my people Israel".'

Then Herod spoke to the Magi privately and learned from them the exact date when the star had appeared. He set them on their way to Bethlehem, and said: 'Go and make exact enquiries about the child, and when you find him, bring back word to me, so that I too can go and worship him.'

After the audience with the king, they set out, and the

star which they had seen in the East went ahead of them until it came to rest above the place where the child was. When they saw the star they were glad and their joy was unbounded. They entered the house, and saw the child with Mary his mother, and fell on their knees and worshipped him; and they opened their treasures and offered him gifts of gold, frankincense and myrrh. Then, as they were warned in a dream not to return to Herod, they took a different route back into their own country.

(*Mt 2:1-12*)

Reflection

There is at least a superficial resemblance between these two events. The queen of Sheba comes with a great retinue, with camels and with precious gifts to visit Solomon, the son of David, and asks him questions which he answers for her. The Magi come to Jerusalem, doubtless with a retinue and camels—how else could they have made the journey?—certainly with precious gifts; and they ask Herod a question: Where is the new-born king of the Jews? Presumably they thought he was a new-born son of Herod, or the question would have been tactless and dangerous.

Herod himself is not another Solomon. He is unable to answer the question. Having no new-born son of his own, he gathers that the question must refer to the Messiah. So he questions the religious experts. Herod does not embody wisdom: he has no ideal home exhibition to take the Magi's breath away, and the cunning which he shows in his attempt to trick them misfires. He is the unworthy heir of the throne of David and Solomon, because he does not execute justice and righteousness. Instead he slaughters innocent children. The Magi do not offer their gifts to him.

They go to Bethlehem and find Jesus. There again they find no ideal home exhibition, but what they found may have taken their breath away—if the 'home' they found was still the cattle-shed and the child's cradle still the manger. But they did find there the Wisdom of God incarnate. If Mary held the Child in her lap while the Magi adored him, she was then the Seat of Wisdom—and the tableau shows the best of Gentile wisdom—philosophers and ascetics who won the praise of Aristotle—kneeling before Wisdom incarnate, enthroned in the lap of Mary, the seat of Wisdom.

As yet, he was not able to answer all their questions for them. But later on, in the temple, he answered the questions of all comers; and when he had reduced them all to silence, he himself raised the question, How can the Messiah be both David's son and his Lord? The question implied that the new Solomon would be greater than the old. And on another occasion, he said to the Jews (Mt 12:42): 'At the Judgment the queen of Sheba will rise up against this generation and condemn it; for she came from the ends of the earth to hear the wisdom of Solomon, and now, here is a greater than Solomon!' This was exemplified at the time of his birth, when the Magi came from the ends of the earth, but Herod and the chief priests and scribes did not even make the five-mile journey from Jerusalem to see for themselves.

As St Paul was to say later, the Wisdom of God looks like folly to men. God seems to want to shock us! We can recognise his wisdom only by becoming humble.

Prayer

Teach us, O heavenly Father, to be humble enough to recognise in the manger and on the cross the Power of God and the Wisdom of God. Lift the veils from our eyes, so that we may see. Through our Lord Jesus Christ your Son, who lives and reigns with you in the unity of the Holy Spirit, and is God, world without end. Amen.

22

Frankincense and myrrh

The Wealth of the Pagan Rome

The kings of the earth who shared her couch and her luxury will weep and lament over her, when they see the smoke of her conflagration. They will stand afar off through terror at the sight of her torments and cry: 'Alas, alas for the Great City, Babylon the mighty city! For in one brief hour your doom has come!'

Then too the merchants of the earth will weep and grieve over her, because no one now will buy their wares —their cargoes of gold and silver, gems and pearls, linen and silks, purple and scarlet, fragrant timber of every kind, carvings in ivory, treasures made of precious wood and bronze and iron and marble, cinnamon, spice and perfumes, myrrh and incense, wine and oil, fine flour and wheat, cattle and sheep, horses and chariots, slaves and human souls. 'All, all are gone from you,' they will say, 'the ripe fruit of your soul's desire! All your glory and splendour are vanished, never to return!' The traders in all this merchandise who grew rich from her will stand far off through terror at the sight of her torments. Weeping and grieving, they will cry: 'Alas, alas for the Great City that was dressed in fine linen and purple and scarlet, and sparkled with gold and gems and pearls! Alas that in one brief hour so much wealth has been ruined!'

And every ship's captain and seaman and sailor and all whose livelihood is from the sea will stand and watch from a distance the smoke of her conflagration; and they will cry: 'What city was like the Great City?' They will throw dust on their heads and cry out with tears and lamentations: 'Alas, alas for the Great City, from whose wealth all who had ships on the sea grew rich! For in one brief hour she has become a ruin!'

But exult, O heaven, and all you saints, apostles and prophets, exult over her! For God has vindicated your cause against her!

Then a mighty angel took up a huge stone like a millstone and hurled it into the sea. 'So,' he said, 'shall the Great City of Babylon be hurled down and vanish without a trace! No more will the sound of harpists and minstrels, pipers and trumpeters, be heard in you! No craftsman of any trade will be found in you; no more will the light of lamps be seen in you; the voices of bridegroom and bride will be heard in you no more! For your merchants were the princes of the earth; and all the nations were seduced by your sorceries.' For the blood of prophets and saints was found upon her, the blood of all who were slain on the earth.

After this I heard the sound of a great throng in heaven crying: 'Alleluia! Victory and glory and power belong to our God, for his judgments are true and just! He has condemned the great harlot who corrupted the earth with her fornication, and he has avenged upon her the blood of his saints!' Then they cried a second time: 'Alleluia! Yes, the smoke goes up from her ruins for ever and ever!'

Then the twenty-four elders and the four living creatures fell down before God seated upon his throne and adored him with cries of 'Amen! Alleluia!' And a voice came from the throne, saying: 'Give praise to our God, all you who serve him and revere him, both great and small!'
(Apoc 18:9-19:5)

The Gifts of the Magi

After the audience with the king, the Magi set out, and the star which they had seen in the East went ahead of them until it came to rest above the place where the child was. When they saw the star they were glad and their joy was unbounded. They entered the house, and saw the child with Mary his mother, and fell on their knees and worshipped him; and they opened their treasures and offered gifts of gold, frankincense and myrrh. *(Mt 2:9-11)*

Reflection

The Seer of the Apocalypse looks forward to the destruction of Rome, which he calls by the symbolic name of Babylon, and shows how the judgment of men conflicts with the judgment of heaven: the merchants lament the destruction of the principal market for their gold and silver, myrrh and incense, cattle and slaves; but the angels in heaven rejoice that the capital of idolatry and immorality has been overthrown.

The same contrast can be seen in the infancy narratives, where the angels sing 'Glory to God in the highest,' but Herod attempts to kill the Child.

The Magi share in the joy of the angels, but their gifts resemble the merchandize of the traders in the Apocalypse. They also resemble the gifts of the queen of Sheba, who was led to the court of Solomon in the first place by her economic interests. The unadorned fact of her visit may be that she was a camel dealer who came to Jerusalem to make a trade pact with Solomon, and while staying with him took the opportunity to ask him a few conundrums and look over his domestic arrangements. Perhaps the Magi too had other interests besides their astronomy and came to prepare the way for mercantile links with the new king of Israel. At all events, the nature of their gifts suggests that they had not yet understood the nature of Christ's kingdom. Gold, frankincense and myrrh were gifts appropriate to another king like the first Solomon. But Christ was not destined to overthrow Rome and raise up Jerusalem to the status of imperial city and centre of the world luxury-trade.

In quite a different way, the gifts of the Magi were appropriate—particularly if (as has been recently suggested) the word normally translated 'gold' really stands for a Phoenician word meaning another aromatic gum.[1] In that case, the Magi brought three fragrant spices; and just as the swaddling-clothes in the cave of the Nativity prefigure the winding-sheet in which Jesus was wrapped at his burial, so the rich gift of spices will prefigure the princely gift of 'myrrh and aloes, about a hundred pound's weight' which Nicodemus brought to the tomb (Jn 19:30). The Magi themselves had no idea of this, but unconsciously they helped to strengthen the amazing resemblances between the circumstances of Christ's birth and of his burial, when he returned to the womb of the earth to be reborn at the resurrection—a thing which the same Nicodemus imagined impossible when he first heard of it (cf. Jn 3:4).

If the gifts of the Magi show a misunderstanding of Christ's kingdom and perhaps a dubious motive in coming to him, we should not say, in contemplating this scene: 'Unfortunately, I have no gold or precious spices, so what can I offer instead?' We should ask: 'The kingdom of

---

[1] Cf. G. Ryckmans in the 'Revue Biblique, 58 (1951) pp. 372-76.

Christ being what it is, a spiritual kingdom, what gifts should I offer him, and what royal gift should I hope to receive in return?'

Prayers

Take, O Lord, and receive my memory, my understanding and my will; take them and guide them by thy grace! Give me thy love and thy grace. With these I am rich enough.

Protect us, O Lord, from the fascinations of wealth; give us the wisdom to see earthly events as the angels see them; and establish your kingdom on earth — a kingdom of justice, love and peace.

23

The suffering of the Innocents

Their Deaths a Warning

At that time, some men arrived who told Jesus of the Galileans whose blood Pilate had mingled with their sacrifices. He said to them: 'Do you imagine, because these Galileans suffered this fate, that they were greater sinners than the other Galileans? No, I tell you; but unless you do penance, you will all perish like them. And what of those eighteen men who were killed at Siloam when the tower fell on them—do you imagine they were the worst offenders of all the inhabitants of Jerusalem? No, I tell you; but unless you do penance, you will all perish like them.' *(Lk 13:1-5)*

Their Deaths a Portent

After the Magi had gone, an angel of the Lord appeared to Joseph in a dream. 'Rise up,' he said, 'and take the child and his mother, and seek refuge in Egypt. Remain there until I tell you. Herod intends to search for the child, to do away with him.'

Joseph therefore rose up and took the child and his mother by night and made his way into Egypt, where he remained until the death of Herod. Thus was fulfilled the word spoken by the Lord through his prophet, when he said: 'From Egypt I called my son.'

When Herod saw that he had been tricked by the Magi, enraged beyond measure, he sent his men and killed all male children of two years and under in Bethlehem itself and in all its neighbourhood, reckoning from the date he had obtained from the Magi. Then was fulfilled the word spoken through the prophet Jeremiah, when he said: 'A voice was heard in Ramah, wailing and loud lamentation; the voice of Rachel bewailing her children, refusing all comfort, because they are gone.'

After the death of Herod, an angel of the Lord appeared in a dream to Joseph in Egypt, and said: 'Rise up, take the child and his mother, and go into the land of Israel; for those who sought to kill the child are dead.' Joseph therefore rose up and took the child and his mother and set out for the land of Israel. (*Mt 2:13-21*)

Reflection

This part of the Christmas story does not contribute to the Christmas atmosphere, except by way of contrast. The fine tableau of the Adoration of Christ by the Magi is quickly upset, the participants scatter, and Bethlehem becomes a scene of bloodshed and mourning—as in the days of the Babylonian exile, when the deportees gathered at Bethlehem, and Jeremiah pictured Rachel, who died in childbirth near Bethlehem, as weeping again over the desolation of the tribe of Benjamin. The contrast suggests some reflections on human happiness and suffering.

First, the moments of great happiness and peace—how rare and brief they are! The gifts of the Holy Spirit are love, joy and peace. But even the holy family did not live an idyllic life of unbroken love and joy and peace, flowing on smoothly and untroubled. We are asking too much of our human condition, which is only an interim and a period of trial, if we expect it to be a condition of uniform joy and peace. Love is by far the most durable of the three. And curiously, love requires adversity and tribulation and suffering, if it is to remain fresh and grow in depth. If peace, prosperity and affluence go on too long, men and women become profoundly uneasy, secretly despise themselves, and begin to react in various anti-social ways. It seems as if moments of great happiness can only be achieved and accepted if they are surrounded on either side by pain and toil and effort. So it was in the life of the holy family. Before the birth of Jesus, Mary and Joseph went through the painful crisis of the discovery of her pregnancy; and soon after, they had to pack up and flee by night into exile.

When they had fled, the children of other fathers and mothers were slaughtered by command of Herod. Here we can hardly avoid asking ourselves, How could God permit such a thing? Were they not innocent? And was not this bloodshed useless? Again, it is a lesson about our human condition: the sins of one man *do* bring sufferings on others. Each man's sins are not visited solely on his own head, as Ezekiel would have liked to believe (cf. Ez 18). The children did not suffer this fate because they were, or would have grown up to be, worse sinners than the other inhabitants of Bethlehem. They died as a result of the sins of others, and are a warning, like the Galileans whose blood Pilate mingled with their sacrifices: 'Unless you do penance, you will all perish like them!' That is why we cannot wash our hands of the conduct of others and say: 'If they want to wallow in sin, that is their own affair.' Sin is not a private affair. It recoils on innocent third parties—as is particularly evident when the greed and ambition of politicians leads to war.

But if the sins of men are not private, nor are their virtues and sacrifices. The wrath of Herod caused the death of these innocents, but Christ's death caused their salvation. Christian tradition has surely been right in regarding the innocents as the victims of the first Christian persecution: the tyrant tried to stamp out Christianity by cutting off their lives. They had no choice in the matter, it is true (any more than we have in whether we contract original sin); but they died for Christ and because of Christ—who, we can be sure, has saved them.

The contemplation of these scenes should help us to be reconciled to our lot. God did not make everything smooth and easy for his own Son, when he came into this world. Why should *we* expect to be treated better?

Prayer

Teach us, heavenly Father, through these mysteries, to accept our lot, to welcome sufferings and tribulations, and to find peace and love in the midst of our trials. Through our Lord Jesus Christ your Son, who lives and reigns with you in the unity of the Holy Spirit, and is God, world without end. Amen.

Note: The reason why St Luke omitted the Visit of the Magi and its sequel may be that he did not wish, at this point, to raise difficult questions about the justice of God.

24

The New Beginning

Out of Egypt

And the Lord said to Moses in Midian, 'Go back to Egypt; for all the men who were seeking your life are dead.' So Moses took his wife and his sons and set them on an ass, and went back to the land of Egypt; and in his hand Moses took the rod of God.

And the Lord said to Moses, 'When you go back to Egypt, see that you do before Pharaoh all the miracles which I have put in your power; but I will harden his heart, so that he will not let the people go. And you shall say to Pharaoh, "Thus says the Lord, Israel is my first-born son, and I say to you, Let my son go that he may serve me; and if you refuse to let him go, behold, I will slay your first-born son".' *(Exod 4:19-23)*

I have called my Son

An angel of the Lord appeared to Joseph in a dream. 'Rise up,' he said, 'take the child and his mother, and seek refuge in Egypt. Remain there until I tell you; Herod intends to search for the child, to do away with him.' So he rose up and took the child and his mother by night and made his way into Egypt, where he remained until the death of Herod. Thus was fulfilled the word spoken by the Lord through his prophet, when he said: 'From Egypt I called my son.' (*Mt 2:13-15*)

Reflection

The evangelist was convinced that with Jesus the history of Israel began all over again. Therefore in writing the beginning of Jesus' history, he was writing a new Genesis and a new Exodus, for Genesis and Exodus narrate the beginnings of Israel according to the flesh. The opening words of St Matthew's gospel are: 'The book of genesis of Jesus Christ.' As the evangelist believed that history follows a cyclic movement, he expected to find correspondences between the events of Genesis and Exodus and the events of Jesus' infancy. He did find them. In fact, he found so many that modern scholars have suspected him of inventing incidents for the infancy narratives, to match the events of Genesis and Exodus. The supposition of this criticism is of course that God does *not* reveal his hand by making his later intervention conform to the pattern of his earlier ones—which is exactly the opposite of the supposition which guided the evangelist.

Jesus is born like a stranger and a pilgrim in the promised land, more homeless than Abraham. Like Jacob and Joseph he goes down into Egypt. Like Joseph he receives the homage of his brethren, the shepherds of Bethlehem. An attempt is made by a tyrant to take the child's life; but like Moses Jesus is saved, though other children perish. Then at the express command of God, Jesus, like Israel, leaves Egypt and returns to the land of Israel. The resemblances are striking enough; but they are not forced. It is not famine that drives the holy family to go into

Egypt. They do not become slaves while there. They receive gifts from the Gentiles (the Magi) before entering Egypt, not before leaving. Jesus does not come to the attention of the rulers of Egypt. There are no plagues. The holy family has no difficulty in leaving. There is no theophany on the way back.

Why did God will that the holy family should go down into Egypt? It can hardly have been simply to make the typological point that the history of Israel was beginning again. Perhaps it was a further warning to the Jews, like the massacre of the innocents: their rejection of the Messiah would not only bring punishment on them as a people, but would drive him out to the Gentiles. The Flight into Egypt is itself a type of what was to happen in the apostolic age, when the Jews as a whole said No to the gospel, and it spread among the Gentiles—at Alexandria among other places, though how it arrived there we do not know.

The Flight into Egypt was not a lesson for Israel at the time when it occurred, since the departure and return of the holy family remained unknown. Perhaps the narrative of it was used as a warning in the appeal to the Jews of the apostolic generation. For us too it remains a warning: if we do not make Christ welcome, he will get up and go —to Africa perhaps, or South America.

Prayers

Come, Lord Jesus, and make your home in our land! Consecrate us to the truth, and unite us all in a bond of peace, so that when our earthly pilgrimage is over, we may all come to see you in the glory which you had with your Father before the world began. Come, Lord Jesus!

Almighty and merciful Father, draw our hearts upwards by the gravitation of love towards the heavenly Jerusalem where our names are written, that where our Lord and Master is, there we may also be, for ever and ever. Amen.